MW01294182

THE WORD OF GOD

THE WORD OF GOD

God Shammgod

G

GALLERY BOOKS

New York   Amsterdam/Antwerp   London
Toronto   Sydney/Melbourne   New Delhi

G

Gallery Books
An Imprint of Simon & Schuster, LLC
1230 Avenue of the Americas
New York, NY 10020

For more than 100 years, Simon & Schuster has championed authors and the stories they create. By respecting the copyright of an author's intellectual property, you enable Simon & Schuster and the author to continue publishing exceptional books for years to come. We thank you for supporting the author's copyright by purchasing an authorized edition of this book.

No amount of this book may be reproduced or stored in any format, nor may it be uploaded to any website, database, language-learning model, or other repository, retrieval, or artificial intelligence system without express permission. All rights reserved. Inquiries may be directed to Simon & Schuster, 1230 Avenue of the Americas, New York, NY 10020 or permissions@simonandschuster.com.

Copyright © 2025 by God Shammgod

All rights reserved, including the right to reproduce this book or portions thereof in any form whatsoever. For information, address Gallery Books Subsidiary Rights Department, 1230 Avenue of the Americas, New York, NY 10020.

First Gallery Books hardcover edition September 2025

GALLERY BOOKS and colophon are registered trademarks of Simon & Schuster, LLC

Simon & Schuster strongly believes in freedom of expression and stands against censorship in all its forms. For more information, visit BooksBelong.com.

For information about special discounts for bulk purchases, please contact Simon & Schuster Special Sales at 1-866-506-1949 or business@simonandschuster.com.

The Simon & Schuster Speakers Bureau can bring authors to your live event. For more information or to book an event, contact the Simon & Schuster Speakers Bureau at 1-866-248-3049 or visit our website at www.simonspeakers.com.

Interior design by Julia Jacintho

Manufactured in the United States of America

10 9 8 7 6 5 4 3 2 1

Library of Congress Control Number: 2025936078

ISBN 978-1-6680-6465-8
ISBN 978-1-6680-6467-2 (ebook)

To my mom, Adrienne Wells

I'm so New York, I got robbed in the *second grade*.

Man, who the hell gets robbed when they're *seven years old*? ME.

Naturally, this took place in Brooklyn. The *old* Brooklyn. Don't picture no smoothie shops or whatever. This was early '80s Crown Heights. The height of the crack era. Reaganomics. Timberlands and gold caps. Kangol hats. Crooklyn, New York. The fuck is a *condo*? We're talking about a different world. A different galaxy from now. Nobody was ordering no Oat Milk lattes, you feel me? They were out here robbing babies, son.

Let me set the scene for you. It's gray. It's *cold*. I'm walking my younger brother and sister to school—I'm big, bro, even though I'm only seven. My sister, she's five, so I always have to drop her off at kindergarten in the morning. My brother, he's like three. He's not doing too much. He's more like our puppy at that point. "Yo—sit! Stay! Be quiet! Good boy."

Now, on this particular morning, I had a little change in my pocket, so we decided to make a detour and stop at White Castle. Burgers for breakfast. We living the dream.

Now, you might be asking yourself: How does a seven-year-old have a little change in his pocket? *You get it from your mom, Shamm? You got an allowance?* Son, I ain't have no damn allowance. You think this is *The Cosby Show*? I'm seven years old. I'm so New York I had a *job*.

I used to sweep up the floors at the West Indian restaurant around the corner from our apartment. I was doing that since I was six. The broom was bigger than me. And we're not exactly on the books, you know what I'm saying? Health and Safety don't need to know about it. You just post up in the spot after school while you listen to the OGs shooting the shit. That's where you get your little introductory education to the world, you feel me? I'm talking about the *real* world. Not the one you learn about in school. You soak up that knowledge and you keep the place clean. Maybe you get a free beef patty with some coco bread. Then at the end of the night, the boss slides you a little pocket money in a handshake on the way out the door. We're not hurting nobody. Simple.

So I remember on that particular morning when we were treating ourselves to some White Castle, we had enough money for like five of them little mini cheeseburgers and a small fry.

Now, I can already hear you saying it . . .

Shamm, that don't sound too nutritional.

Listen, man. You're not really from New York if you weren't eating White Castle before elementary school. If you never ate french fries in the parking lot of a White Castle before going to P.S. 2-0-whatever, you're from the *other* New York, son.

Anyway, we get these burgers and head out toward school. And this bag is steaming, man. It's piping hot. Those little grilled onions—oh my God. You *know* that smell. The winter breeze is wafting those golden-brown crispy-ass french fries into the air, and as we're walking along Utica Avenue, everybody around us is salivating. People waiting for the bus. People sitting on stoops. Their heads are turning. They're sniffing the air. We can't *wait* to get to the playground and eat these burgers, right?

We're walking, we're talking. Life is good.

Then, out of nowhere, this random dude walks up on us. And he's looking at the bag, real curious.

He's like, "Hey, young fella. Is that . . is that *White* Castle?"

He's pointing at the bag, like it's . . *interesting* or something. Like it's mad intriguing to him. He's examining it like a rare artifact.

So now I'm holding the bag up, real confused, like, "Huh? This bag right here?"

He's looking at us real friendly. He's smiling. He says, "Yeah, that bag right there. Is that one of them *White Castle* burgers?"

I said, "Yeah."

He said, "Ahhh. I *heard* about them. Hey, can I ask you a favor?"

I said, "We gotta go to school."

He said, "Wait, wait, wait. Would you mind if I smell your bag for a second?"

Now I'm just befuddled. I'm seven years old, son! I'm looking at him like, *Smell my bag?*

He's like, "Just a sniff. It smells so good. Please?"

And he's holding out his hand, all innocent, like: *Come on, son. Give a poor man a sniff.*

I'm holding up the bag, and we're all looking at it. Me, the random dude, my brother, my sister. And that bag is steaming. It's glowing.

And in that split second of hesitation . . .

Whapppppp.

The dude snatches the bottom half of the bag right out my hand. He hit me with the kung fu karate swipe. *Gimmie that, son.*

He takes off.

Before I can even process what's happening, dude is *gone.*

Gone with the wind, son.

This man *hamburgled* a couple of little kids at eight o' clock in the morning on Utica Ave. I mean, *picture me.* I'm standing in the middle of the street, still holding the handle of this White Castle bag. My stomach is growling. I'm speechless. And my brother and sister are just looking up at me. They got tears streaming down their little faces. They're *bawling.*

Saddest sight you've ever seen in your life.

My sister is like, "I *really* wanted them burgers too."

She's got the snot coming out and everything. Her bottom lip sticking out. Quivering.

Me? I didn't shed a single tear, man.

I just looked up at the clouds like, *Oh, alright, God. I see now. I see what it is out here in these streets. You're teaching me, huh? I'm listening.*

Welcome to New York City, young fella.

Welcome to the *world.*

"God *Shamm*god?"

"That name can't be real."

"You made that shit up."

"You think you're special or something?"

I've been hearing it all my life. But that's really my government name. I was actually the second God Shammgod. My father was the original. Like a lot of the OGs of his era, coming up in the 1960s and '70s, he was an activist, an intellectual, a street philosopher, a fighter, a boxing trainer, a Muslim, and one hell of a disciplinarian. If you're familiar with the Black Panthers, then you got a taste of what my father and my friends were all about. To them, Black Power was not some catchphrase on a T-shirt. It wasn't no fashion statement. It was what they were living every single day, for real. My father was actually a member of the Five Percent Nation. If you know about the Five Percenters, then you already know. If you don't know, then you don't need to know. You feel me?

One of the first lessons you learn, say, when you're sweeping the floors of the West Indian joint, is that when strangers start coming around asking too many questions, the best response is "I don't know nothing about that."

Sometimes you just gotta accept the mystery.

When I was little, my father was in the streets. There's no sugarcoating it. He wasn't a bad man in any real sense of the word. He wasn't a killer. But he was out there hustling. And when you're out there hustling, it's only a matter of time before you're dead or in jail. When I was about six years old, he got put away for robbery, and I had to become the man of the house.

Lucky for me, my father taught me two very valuable lessons before he went to prison: knowledge of self and discipline. The first lesson is going to take this whole book for you to really understand. The second is simple. When you do something, you do it all the way. We're not quitting and we're not crying. That goes all the way back to my first memory in life, as a matter of fact. When I was five years old, I was enamored with this pendant that my father was always wearing on his jacket. It was the Five Percenters symbol. The moon and the stars and the 7. It was mysterious and powerful to me. I always wanted to hold it in my hands. We were at my grandma's house one night, and I asked him if I could borrow it. He was like, "Alright, but this is not a toy. This *stands* for something. It's sacred. Don't lose it."

Of course, I was playing outside in the backyard, and I lost it in the grass.

I went back inside. If I'd had a tail, it would have been between my legs.

"You lost the pendant?"

I'm stammering. I'm trying to explain, like, "Well, what happened was . . ."

My father looks me dead in my eyes, and with the most I'm-not-to-be-trifled-with tone of voice, which he made famous all over New York City long before I was born, he tells me, "Go back out there. Don't come inside until you have that pendant."

Now, mind you, this pendant is the size of a quarter. I go out into the backyard, and the sun is starting to set already, so it's like trying to find a needle in a hackstack. I'm looking for one hour, two hours, three hours. Nothing. The sun goes down. It's dark. I can't see a thing. I start crying. I'm never going to find this thing. It's hopeless.

I start to go back inside, and right as I get to the back door, my father is waiting there.

"You have my pendant?"

I'm blubbering. Snot coming out. "Nah, I . . ."

"Did I tell you it was sacred?"

"Yeah, but . . ."

"Did I tell you not to stop until you found it?"

"Yeah, but . . ."

"I trusted you with it. No point in crying. Just find it."

At that moment, I have this premonition. Like I can see the future. And do you know what I saw? I saw an ass-whuppin' in my future, clear as day. And the worst part was that I knew that it was rightfully deserved. Those ones sting the most, don't they? When you're thinking: *Damn. I'd whupp my ass too.*

So I turn around and go back out into the yard. I get down on my hands and knees like a dog. And it's like a switch flipped inside me. This is going to sound crazy, but I can still vividly remember that I transformed in that moment. It was like I stopped being a little kid that night. Five years old, but a grown man. The crying stopped. And I just had this inner fire, like: *Nah, fuck this. We're done with the kiddie shit. I am not coming inside until I find this pendant. I don't care if it takes me twenty-four hours. I am going to find it.*

I think it took me six hours. But I found the needle in the haystack. When I brought it back inside and gave it to my father, I was a different person. I carried that lesson with me my entire life, and it was a lesson I needed at that exact moment. Because six months later, my father wasn't there anymore; he was locked up in a cage. My mother was beside herself, drinking way too much just to deal with the stress. I had a younger brother and sister to take care of.

What you have to understand about Brooklyn is, in that era, it was not about the music, or the culture, or the pizza, or even the ball players. That was the other boroughs. Don't let anybody tell you any different. They're trying to rewrite history. No, at that time, Brooklyn was about one thing above all else: fighting. It was in the DNA of the streets. It was in the *atmosphere*. When you walked out the door in the morning, you were *tensed up*. Every fiber in your body was ready for a fight. Walking down the block, nobody was smiling. Not even your own people. God's honest truth, I barely even remember watching basketball or football or even cartoons on TV. Hooping? What do I care about that for? It ain't relevant. You can't hit nobody. Cartoons? That's some baby shit. Maybe I can sit through a few minutes of *He-Man*. All I remember watching on TV was kung fu movies and wrestling. I'm talking the *real* wrestling, not that fake Olympic stuff. I'm talking *WWF*—Ricky the Dragon Steamboat, the Mouth of the South Jimmy Hart, Macho Man

Randy Savage—*Oh YEAH, brother, can ya DIG IT?* Ric Flair with the alligator loafers and the Rolex that cost more than your momma's house. Those were my heroes, not Dr. J.

That was just the wavelength we were on in the hood. We could relate to that energy. Listen, this is *Crown Heights. Flatbush. Bed-Stuy.* We're not really trying to watch somebody throwing a nice crisp bounce pass, you know what I'm saying? We're not trying to sit in front of the TV watching Kevin McHale shooting free throws, nah-mean? That's soft. We about that *action.* We're trying to suplex a little cousin through a plastic picnic table or something. We're trying to do a flying elbow drop off the back of the couch onto an unsuspecting little brother, you feel me? Larry Bird isn't really relevant to us like that. But the Macho Man? The Macho Man is the American Dream. He's the baddest man on the planet, with the baddest bitch at his side, the lovely *Miss Elizabeth.* He's got the flyest clothes—the cowboy hat, the pink and black leather jacket, the crazy sunglasses, the swagger. That was our *guy.*

In Brooklyn, basketball wasn't really cool like that. Brawling was cool. In the first grade, you had your different crews—almost like little gangs—and it was always the Autobots versus the Decepticons. Like from *The Transformers.* I was with the Autobots. You would meet up in the park after school and get after it. No weapons or nothing, just throwing hands. You're telling me you never seen a twelve-on-twelve battle royale with *kinnygarteners?* Then you're not really from New York. You're from the *other* New York. Point blank period.

You never knew when a fight might break out. Half the time it wasn't even *over* nothing. No beef. No incident. It was just for fun. Like a hobby. In Harlem, they're playing pickup at the park. In Brooklyn, we're out here choke-slamming kids, man. Wherever, whenever. PE class. Recess. Let's get it. Put a dude in a sleeper hold until he passed out or he *tapped out*, and then it was like, "Alright, you had enough? Are we straight? Alright, I'll see you tomorrow."

I've seen motherfuckers get put in a figure-four leg lock at the bodega.

That's Brooklyn.

I've seen motherfuckers get Bruce Lee roundhouse-karate-kicked at the cookout.

That's Brooklyn.

I've seen motherfuckers get crossface-chicken-winged after math class.

In Brooklyn, it was a 24/7 no-holds-barred royal rumble every day.

Friends? In Brooklyn, you didn't have friends. You had sparring partners. When that alarm clock went off in the morning, it was like you heard Michael Buffer's voice in your head. Remember the homie in the tuxedo who used to pump up the crowd before a big fight? *Ding. Ding. Ding.*

"*Ladies* and gentlemen . . . Are . . . you . . . *ready*? Brooklyn, New York! I *said* . . . ARE . . . YOU . . . *RRRRRRRRRRREADY*??"

You had to be ready to rumble, son. And I didn't know it then, but my environment was preparing me very well for what was to come. It was giving me those calluses that I needed to survive. Funny how life works like that, right? In the moment, it always feels like chaos. But when you look back on it with enough distance, everything makes perfect sense. See, with my dad locked up, everything kind of went off the rails for our family. I remember going to visit him in jail, and the first couple of times it was just surreal. I couldn't really process it. I remember wanting to hug him, and I couldn't. That really messed me up. I mean, my father is behind glass. *My* father. Not just any regular father. We're talking about this strong black man who was damn near invincible to me. You're telling me I can talk to him, but I can't touch him? Do you know what that does to a kid? I remember asking the prison guard, "I can't give my dad a hug?"

And he just shook his head no.

I was like, "Why can't I just go back there with him for a minute? I'll come right back. I'm not gonna cause any problems."

Nah. All I could do was touch the glass.

That image is burned into my brain. It filled me with this anxiety that's really hard to explain. It's the only thing that I fear, to this day. I'd rather be dead than be trapped in a cage. I'm forty-nine years old, and it gives me the chills just thinking about it. I'd rather be dead than not have my *freedom*.

I love my father, but it got to the point where I didn't even want to go see him in that state, because it hurt me so much, and I could tell that it hurt him so much. One day, I told my mother that I didn't want to go to the prison anymore. I couldn't take it. I used to have a whole father. Now all I have is this ghost behind the Plexiglas. For a long time, I blamed him for all the pain that I felt, even though it was a lot more complicated than that. I just thought: *You were my hero, man. You are my hero, still. But you left me alone with the wolves. Why?*

Around that time, my mother started drinking more and more. She started smoking more and more. Next thing I know, she's got a new boyfriend. Next thing I know, I got a new stepfather. Next thing I know, it's getting really scary in our apartment.

They started fighting. Verbally, at first. Then ashtrays start hitting the walls, you feel me? Screaming. Glass breaking. Then they started physically fighting. Hair is getting pulled. Punches are getting thrown. Every time you walked through that door, you didn't know what was going to happen. There was always this tension in the air, even during the day. But at night? At night it might get real bad. At night I might have to protect my mother from a grown man. At night I might have to grab a knife from the kitchen. At night I might have to do whatever it takes to make sure that we all make it to tomorrow morning, you understand? I accept it, whatever consequences that come with it are. Because now I'm the protector of my mother and my siblings. I am a little-ass kid, but I am the man of the house.

So some nights, I'm grabbing a steak knife.

Some nights, I'm standing guard in front of her bedroom door.

And this is the point in every hood story where we need to hit the pause button. Because if you're *not* from where we're from, you start jumping to conclusions. You start painting with a broad brush. You start seeing everybody involved as a cliche. Ain't that what you see in every movie about the hood? The pure good guy. The pure bad guy. But the truth is that nobody in this story is all good or all bad. My father wasn't a bad guy. My mother wasn't a bad woman. Part of her was the *best* woman you ever met, as a matter of fact. Ask anybody from my neighborhood, and they got the receipts. They'll tell you. If you were sleeping on the streets, she would let you crash at our house.

"Grab yourself a spot on that couch, baby. You need a blanket?"

If you were hungry, she'd cook you macaroni and cheese like you were her own child. Open-door policy. She was the mom of the whole neighborhood, even when we didn't have a penny to our name. My mother had a pure soul, but a heavy heart, you feel me?

Even my stepfather was not an evil person. He was just a man with some deep issues who was taking care of three children who weren't his own, living paycheck to paycheck and battling his own demons.

When you grow up in the hood, it's hard to hold hate in your heart for anyone, because you know the stress that is weighing down on everybody. In our world, nothing is black and white. It's all gray. So even when I'm talking about *real shit*, please keep in mind that in this story, there are no villains. Only humans.

Some nights, when my mom and stepfather first started drinking and the shit hadn't quite hit the fan yet, I would get up out of the apartment for a while. I'd take my pillow and go off by myself at nine or ten o'clock at night, and I'd go lie on this bench in the alleyway behind our apartment. I used to lie there for hours, just staring up at the sky and crying.

That's when I first started talking to God.

I don't know why, but I always felt this intense connection to God, even when I was young.

I'd ask, "How can I make things better? How can I get my mother and my siblings out of this situation? There has gotta be a way out of this."

I used to lay there in the dark alleyway, staring up at the moon hanging over Harlem, just praying for better days. Praying for a chance. I hadn't even dribbled a basketball yet. I hadn't ever been out of New York City. But I had this vision that I could be something great. Somebody who could change my family's circumstances. Somebody special. God was telling me. He was whispering it to me.

"Please, God. I know you can hear me. I am begging you. Just show me something different. Show me the way."

Around midnight, I would go back inside and check on my mom.

I remember getting halfway up the stairwell and just listening for the muffled sounds coming from behind the door.

Is tonight gonna be a bad night or not?

God, please give me strength. I need you.

If it was quiet, I could go to sleep.

If it was chaos, it was time to be a man.

Sometimes, it's gotta get worse before it can get better.

When I was about to turn ten years old, my stepfather lost his job. Rent came due. Rent came past due. We had to move. "Where we going? Granny's house? Down the block?"

"Nah. We goin' to Harlem to live with your auntie." *Harlem?* To me, that was like saying we were moving to China. "Moms, we don't even speak the same language. I can't understand Harlem dudes."

My aunt's place was on 142nd Street. Uptown, baby. Crime Square. Seven blocks from Rucker Park. Sixteen blocks from *Showtime at the Apollo*. Fifteen blocks from Dapper Dan's boutique. Center of the black universe. At the time, I was ignorant of all that. I didn't know what was going on, or what any of the signs meant. The only culture I knew about was Hulkamania, brother. If I couldn't suplex it or box it, I didn't know what it had to do with me. Day one in Harlem, I was seeing stars. Walking down the block to the corner store for the first time, it was like everything went from black-and-white to Technicolor. It was a whole different world, even aesthetically. In Brooklyn, every sign was hand-painted. In Harlem, everything was glowing neon. In Brooklyn, the music was coming out of somebody's half-broken boom box on a stoop. In Harlem, the subwoofers in the trunk of somebody's Cadillac El Dorado were vibrating the whole block. The style, the energy, the colors, the music, the people. I don't say this to be a hater, I'm just stating facts. I love Brooklyn, but at that time, Brooklyn was depressed. Harlem was vibrant. Brooklyn was meanmugs on every street corner. It was crabs in a bucket. The vibe was, *If I don't know you, I don't need to know you.*

In Harlem, I saw black people smiling on the corner for the first time in my life. I saw black people breathing easy, succeeding, thriving. It's funny because I used to go to these Five Percenter rallies with my father before we went to jail, and the theme was always about black greatness and confidence and success and togetherness. But honestly, I never saw that in my real life in Crown Heights. Brooklyn was the embodiment of that famous Biggie lyric—"Either you're slinging crack rock or you got a wicked jump shot."

But when we moved to Harlem, I saw another way of life. I saw "Black Is Beautiful." I saw hope. I saw greatness. I'm seeing Gucci belts and Louis Vuitton and Coogi sweaters and Hermès and all kinds of clothes I've never seen before and I can't even pronounce. Even the fake Gucci looks real. I tell people all the time, especially the young kids now who think success is all about how many zeroes you got in your bank account: Harlem is the only place in the world where people with ten dollars in their pocket make it look like a hundred. And if you got a thousand? You're looking like a million bucks.

It was breathtaking. I was captivated by the sights and the sounds. I'm seeing Mercedes C300s parked in front of the projects. I'm seeing Reeboks in different colors—I didn't even know you could get 'em in anything but white. I'm seeing drug dealers wearing mink coats and pinkie rings like we're in *GoodFellas*. Dudes getting a fresh lineup just to go to the corner store for a pack of Swishers. I'm seeing hustlers on the corner selling mixtapes. I'm hearing slang I never heard in my life, and the sound of laughter on every block.

I was literally thinking, *Man, what the fuck is so funny?*

Harlem. *That's* what funny. Every man, woman, and *child* in Harlem is funny. They come out the *womb* spitting jokes on their fathers.

But me, I was still Brooklyn to my core. A fish out of water in my Timberlands and my black hoodie. I barely knew how to crack a smile. To me, that shit was *suspicious*. Like: Smiling? What do you want from me? What angle you trying to work here?

Those first couple of weeks in Harlem, I felt so out of place. I was actually taking the train by myself back to Brooklyn every day just to be with my old friends. They'd probably call Child Services on us now, but to me, it was normal. I was on my own. I had to adapt. I'd go back to the block with my grimy Brooklyn friends and I'd be saying, "Man, Harlem is crazy. Everybody's dressed goofy as hell. Dudes be making fun of each other and they don't even wanna fight over it. *Weirdos*, son."

For me, everything changed when I started going to PS92 in Harlem for fifth grade.

I was telling my mom for weeks, "I don't want to go to school with these Harlem kids. Can't I just take the train every morning into Brooklyn and go to my old school?"

I was dreading it. Especially the fashion. For me, clothes were just *clothes*. You get up and you put on whatever. In Harlem, clothes were everything. I showed up the first day of school at PS92 in my Spot-Bilt sneakers. Remember the OJ Simpsons? The clunky black-and-white Spot-Bilt Sonics? I had my flat top with the half-moon part. Two gold caps in my teeth. Hat to the back. I walk into class looking all *militant*. I'm looking like 2Pac in *Juice*. And these Harlem kids are staring back at me like I'm an *alien*. They're pointing down like, "Yo B, where'd you get them shoes? Payless?"

I'm like, "Yeah. *Payless*. What's the problem?"

Everybody's laughing. I didn't even get it. I'm trying to act all tough, but nobody even wants to fight me. In Harlem, you had to be mentally on point at all times. It wasn't about the fists, it was about the wit. I'm *flummoxed*. I'm *wildin'*. I remember I kept saying, "Yo, I'm from *Brooklyn*, son. We don't play out there. I know karate, *son*."

Everybody's like, "Yeah, whatever, *son*. Put them shoes in the trash."

They kept calling me "Dudley." Like the little dude from *Diff'rent Strokes*. They said I looked just like him. They were hitting me with the wildest references I ever heard, and they didn't even have Google. Little kids are coming up with this stuff just off the top of the dome. My head was spinning, man. I'm thinking: I can't survive this shit. I need an *Encyclopaedia Britannica* just to even understand what these Harlem dudes are talking about.

I went home that night and told my moms, "You gotta give me some money to go to the barber. We gotta get rid of this flat top."

Bzzzztttt. Now I'm Pac after *Juice.* "Ma, I need a gold chain for my birthday. I don't even care if it's fake. Just make me look fly."

Thank God, this one dude in class was supercool to me from the jump. I met Mason Betha on the first day of school. A good friend can change your life. A best friend? That's priceless. Mason was one of those kids that was just good at everything. He was street smart *and* book smart. He was so charismatic that you couldn't even call him a nerd. You'd hear all the teachers being like, "You know who y'all need to be like? Y'all need to be more like *Mason.*"

One of the first things he ever said to me was, "Yo B, you play ball?"

I said, "*Ball?* Like basketball? Nah, I don't know nothing about that."

I had never dribbled a basketball in my life. I go to the cafeteria for lunch, and Mason is putting on a show. This little dude is dribbling the ball between his legs, crossing it over, seeing how long he could go for, and the whole lunchroom is cheering him on. I had never seen anything like it. I was in awe. I'm like, "Dang, I wanna do that."

Then we sit down at the lunch table, and this dude starts *rapping*. Freestyling. But not no basic "1-2-1-2, yo, yo, it's MC Mase and I'm in the place." No, no, no. This kid is actually *good*. He's got bars. Everyone's nodding along, and banging on the lunch tables like, "Yoooooo!!! Murda Mase on the mic!"

Then this dude got his library books out—he's reading *Latin* and shit.

No, I'm just playing, but he was probably doing complex mathematics while eating his chicken nuggets. He was just Mr. Do-It-All.

He's like, "Shamm, you want to come to the park tonight? We're meeting up with some shorties."

This little dude got *girls*, too? We *e-leven*.

I'm looking at him in amazement like, "Bro, who *are* you?"

He's smiling at me. And you know this smile. You've *seen* this smile. Matter of fact, the whole world has seen this smile. The one and only Ma$e.

Cue the music.

Now, who's hot, who not?
Tell me who rock, who sell out in the stores?
You tell me who flopped, who copped the blue drop?
Whose jewels got rocks?

God doesn't do coincidence, only providence. Every person that God put in my life, he put there for a good reason. So when we go to the park after school, Ma$e really *does* have some shorties there, because his charisma was like this gravitational pull that made everybody want to be around him. But he also brings along these two kids from the Delanor Projects a few blocks down from us—two hilarious dudes named Cam and Huddy.

Huddy was a natural hype man. He was saying, "Oh, you think Mase is nice? Wait till you hear Cam rapping. He's *stupid*."

Then this kid Cam starts spitting some bars on the spot and *he's* nice with it too.

I'm like: Yo, who *is* this dude? What the hell is going on? Can everybody in Harlem rap?

(Yes.)

Cue the music.

Yo, now I was downtown clubbin', ladies night
Seen shorty she was crazy right
And I approached baby like, "Ma, what's your age and type?"
She looked at me and said, "You's a baby right?"
I told her, I'm eighteen and live a crazy life
Plus I'll tell you what the eighties like

Cam is really Cameron Giles. Later known as the one and only *Cam'ron*.

Now, what you need to understand is that to me, this is just a bunch of random eleven-year-olds I started chilling with. We're trying to go to the bodega and get some chopped cheese and some Now and Laters. That's a good day for us. We don't know *what* the hell life has got in store. At the time, all these dudes were just broke little kids. None of us had ever been to a concert. We had barely ever been out of the city.

Matter of fact, I remember Cam'ron always saying (and you gotta imagine that Cam'ron voice when he says this, because dude sounded like Killa Cam even back then): "Mannnn, I don't really even rap like that. I'm gonna be a ball player. I'm stupid nice with it. I'm getting a scholarship."

Cam was way, way, way better than anyone I'd ever seen at ball at that point. He was like a little Russell Westbrook. He didn't care. He was going straight at dudes. Right to the rim. He actually was *nice nice* at ball. Mase was more like a Pet Beverley. Little agitator. And me, I was just sitting in the bleachers bullshitting, trying to talk to the shorties.

Every street corner I was on, there was somebody who wasn't *somebody* yet. The park on 139th Street was our spot, and it was perfect because I lived on 142nd Street, and Mase was on 133rd and Cam was on 140th. We'd go to that park pretty much every day, to play ball or just to sit around bullshitting. All the time, we'd be hearing dudes saying, "Oh you think Mason and Cam are nice? Nah, they okay. They alright. Who you really gotta hear is this dude Lamont."

Sooner or later, we run into this dude Lamont Coleman at the park. He's dressed fly as hell, even though he's only got two dollars in his pocket. He's got a crowd of people around him. And he is really, *really* nice with it. He's on another level.

At this point, I'm like: Yoooo. What is going *on*? Am I in a movie? Who is *this* fool?

Where's my DJ? Cue the music.

Yo, fuck all the glamours and glitz, I plan to get rich
I'm from New York and never was a fan of the Knicks
And I'm all about expandin' my chips
You mad 'cause I was in the van with your bitch

Real ones know. Lamont Coleman, also known as *Big L.* Just another Top 50 all-time rapper in the park spitting bars on a random Wednesday at St. Nich's Park. Within a few years—when we were around twelve, thirteen, fourteen years old—Big L became the top dog around Harlem, to the point where he couldn't walk down the block or show up at the barbecue without somebody just yelling out, "Yo! Big L! My mans over here is better than you! He got bars!"

You ever seen the old kung fu movies where the samurais are crossing each other's paths and they just give each other a *look,* like: *Alright, little homie, it's on.* That was exactly the way it was. Somebody would have a boom box or start beatboxing or just banging on the picnic table, and all of a sudden it was Big L in a battle rap against Fat Joe. Just impromptu. No cell phones. No cameras. Just people eating Chinese food sitting in the bleachers. One day, this kid shows up to see my man Huddy. He's a little bit older, and everybody is cool with him, talking about: "Oh yeah, this here my man Nasir from Queens. He's *nice* on the mic."

I'm like, alright, whatever. He's talking about, "Y'all know what it is. It's Nasty Nas from Queensbridge. Word is bond, son. Word is bond."

I don't think twice about it. He's cool. Whatever. It's just another kid with a dream. A couple years later, this dude is dropping a little album you might've heard of called *Illmatic*.

Y'all already know what to do! Cue the legend's music!

The street raised me up giving a fuck
I thought Jordans and a gold chain was living it up
I knew the dopes, the pushers, the addicts, everybody
Cut out of class just to smoke blunts and drink Noddy

It's Nas, coming to you live from the BBQ.

What's funny is that a lot of kids reading this now probably don't know the name Big L (God bless the dead). But if you don't know the history of hip-hop then you really need to go to YouTube and educate yourself on one of the best MCs to ever do it. Nas used to say that the first time he ever heard Big L rap, he told himself that he had to quit, because he could never do it at that level. He was so hard that he literally scared Nas to death. True story.

But the scariest of the bunch was this older dude from Yonkers who used to come around sometimes. His name was Earl, and he was gritty. Intense. Real deep voice. The word on the street was that he was homeless as a kid, and his only friends were the stray dogs that he found sleeping with him in abandoned buildings. It sounds like a story from a comic book or something, but it was true. Dude really used to be standing on the corner *barking* at motherfuckers. Literally snarling and shit. *Ruffin'* at gangsters.

He don't *care*. Challenging random dudes to battle him. Earl referred to himself as the Divine Master of the Universe. And he was pretty nice on the mic, but honestly he was so intense and so raw that when we were young he was just basically "homeboy on the corner over there," you know what I'm saying? Every neighborhood got one of these guys. It just so happened that in our neighborhood the crazy Yonkers dude outside the corner store turned out to be one of the biggest legends in hip-hip history.

Earl Simmons.

Also known as the Divine Master of the Universe

Also known as Dark Man X

Also known as the one and only DMX.

Cue the damn music, man.

You think it's a game? You think it's a fuckin' gaaaaaaame?

Come on!!!!

What y'all really want???

What y'all really want?

What? D. M. X.

All these guys were all just *around*. Chilling. Eating fried rice in the park. Smoking Ls. Talking. Debating who's the best rapper, who's the flyest chick, who got the best dope.

People ask me all the time, "Shamm, you really knew those dudes? What was DMX like? What was Nas like?"

They were the exact same dudes you know now, but with no *money*. DMX was really walking around with two pit bulls, snarling at people. Choker chain on with the bald head. Cam was really wearing Carhartt and pink polos fifteen years before anybody was wearing Carhartt and pink polos, walking up to the shorties in the park like, "Hey ma, what's up?"

Jay-Z. Puff. Biggie. Jadakiss. Styles P. Dame Dash. The list is endless. They were just *around*. But just to give you the full picture, when we were kids, we knew Jay more for the *other thing* he was doing than as a rapper. He was still moving those bricks by the O-Z, you feel me? All the lyrics coming from New York City ain't a fairy tale. Every word is a documentary. (Except if we got feds reading.) All these world-changing artists and moguls and producers were just part of the fabric of the neighborhood. We weren't starstruck. We didn't know any different.

I don't say that to be cocky or ungrateful. But at that time, Harlem was the mecca of black culture. No, it was *the culture*. Period. If you were anybody—or if you were *nobody*—you were coming to Harlem to hang out. And to be clear, I was a nobody at that time. I was just the crusty little dude from Brooklyn that Mase and Cam used to bring around. I was real quiet. Real rough around the edges. I didn't trust anybody. Couldn't rap. Couldn't play ball. Didn't want to be in the streets, because of what happened to my father. I just didn't really have my *thing*, you feel me? But I can tell you the exact moment that my life changed.

One day, Mase said the magic words: "Hey, we goin' to the Rucker. It's the All-Star."

I didn't know anything about "the Rucker." I mean, I knew it was a park. But I definitely didn't know what "the All-Star" was all about. But what else do I got to do, right? So I tag along like it's a normal day, thinking we're gonna get a box of hot wings and some Goofy Juices and sit in the park bullshitting and talking to girls. I roll out with my new crew. I didn't know these boys were going to be my *lifelong* crew. It was me, Mase, Zig, Woods, Howie, and Mike, also known as Pretty Boy Mike. We take the 1 train uptown to Rucker Park on 154th, and as soon as we get through the gates of the park it's like . . . It's impossible. It's *live*.

It's straight pandemonium, son. It's like the 1989 version of Mardi Gras and spring break and the BET Awards all rolled into one. At first, I don't even understand what I am witnessing. You got BMWs and Porsches and Mercedes. Bodyguards. Stacks of cash. You got drug dealers and rappers and the finest women I've seen in my life. And then in the middle of all of this, on the basketball court, it's not like any basketball I've ever seen on TV. It's like gladiators in the Roman Colosseum. We're some little kids still, so we're trying to get a better view. We hop up on the gate at first, but it was too far away. We couldn't see the court. So Mase points to this big oak tree, and he's like, "Yo, you think we can climb it without dying?"

We climb it without dying.

Now we're sitting courtside. Fifteen feet in the air. We're in the hood luxury box. And I cannot believe what I am seeing. These dudes are not shooting free throws. They're not doing bounce passes. They're going *crazy*. They're not basketball players. They're artists. Entertainers. They're doing stuff with a basketball that defies the laws of physics, *metaphysics*, gravitation, *thermodynamic* laws. They're breaking them all. I'm in awe. My eyes are buggin' out. There's an older guy running around the court with a bullhorn, and every time somebody crosses somebody over or dunks the ball, he's screaming out like a wrestling announcer: "Ohhhh my GAWD! He *killed* his ass! God bless the dead! Somebody call his momma!"

The crowd was electric. It was like being at a rap concert—only I had never been to a rap concert. Every time somebody got crossed up, it was more like they spit some bars. The crowd was going, "Whoooaaaaaaa *shit! Yooooooo!!!*"

Everybody had an alter ego—like a wrestling name.

Kareem Wilson aka "Pookie."

Malloy Nesmith aka "Future."

Mike Boogie.

Master Rob.

The *Terminator*.

I'm drinking my Grape Goofy Juice, sitting up in this tree like: I didn't know this world existed. I wanna do this. I *need* to do this. I gotta get one of them basketballs, son.

Then something preposterous happened. Something that defied every law of nature: the moment that really changed my life. Mike Boogie went down on one knee, dribbled the ball between his legs, then he put the ball between the defender's legs, pulled it back again, did a little *shimmy* and then hit a three. And ten thousand people in Harlem went absolutely apeshit. But the kicker for me was that I never seen so many girls go crazy before. He hit the three and shorties were literally taking their tops off.

I'm looking at Mase with my eyes bugged out like: "Yoooooooo!!! What???"

I get goose bumps just thinking about it to this day. No cameras. No social media. Just real street basketball, doing it for the love of it. Just the community *showing out*. The energy was infectious. I really thought I was in the center of the universe. Madison Square Garden? We didn't know nothing about that. Same city, different planet. Rucker Park was *our* Madison Square Garden. That was the promised land.

I was telling Mase and all my boys, the whole walk home, "Yo, I'm gonna be out there someday. That's gonna be me."

Then I went home that night and I told my mother—I literally said the words: "Mom! I need to play this sport called basketball."

And I remember she said, "You gonna stay out of trouble?"

I said, "Yeah, if I play basketball I swear I'll stay out of trouble."

She said, "Whatever you want then, baby."

I don't know how, but I got a basketball in my hands the next day. I don't know if I stole it or borrowed it. But I got one. I was twelve years old when I played basketball for the first time. In this day and age, kids got fucking *shoe deals* at twelve. They got a social media following. They got college coaches hitting them up in the DMs. Nowadays, if you're not already good by twelve, you're *washed*. It's over for you, son. Me, I was out there after all the big homies had left the park so I wouldn't be embarrassed, just trying to put the ball between my legs, like—*damn, this is a lot harder than it looks at the Rucker.* Ball bouncing away, dudes smoking Ls sitting on the bleachers, shaking their heads like— *Yo, Dudley trying to play ball now?*

I sucked. I was *ass*. I had no money. No future. I was a nobody.

Within two years, I was the number-one-ranked freshman in New York City.

Within three years, I was a hood celebrity. Everybody in Harlem knew the name "Shammgod."

Within four years, I was taking pictures with Biggie Smalls. I was riding around in limos with Puffy. I was treating the whole hood to McDonald's. I was teaching Kobe how to dribble. I had people saying that I had the best handle since the Messiah.

In the snap of a finger, I had received the one thing that I asked God for when I was lying on that bench in the alleyway. When I was just a lost little kid, crying my eyes out.

I got the best gift you can ask for when you're born into poverty.

A way out.

Now, you might be asking yourself: How did all this shit happen so fast?

It don't seem possible, Shamm. You telling tall tales? How do you go from never touching *a basketball to your name ringing out in the streets in just two years?*

Well, let me ask *you* a question. Do you know how you get to Carnegie Hall?

It ain't the A train, son.

There's only one way to get there.

Practice.

Practice.

3

Dribbling is not about the ball.

This is the mistake that everybody makes. Forget the ball. Forget your hands. Dribbling has nothing to do with what's going on with your hands. It's got nothing to do with the person standing in front of you, slapping the pavement, talking shit. That's just your first victim. He might as well be a traffic cone. Nah, see, dribbling is not even about what's happening *right now*, in the moment. Dribbling exists on a different plane. It's spiritual. It's metaphysical, son.

I'm not being funny. If you're laughing, then your ass definitely don't got a handle. See, you still exist in this material realm. That's your first mistake. You're in the world of ego and worry and nerves and pride. If you want to have true handle, you need to shed all that baggage. When you're dribbling—when you're *really* dribbling—your spirit is someplace else. "You" don't exist. That ain't a metaphor. If you are *here*, right now, in this dank-ass gym or this park or at Madison Square Garden, with the ball in your hand, thinking about what's going to happen next, or what dope "move" you're doing to pull out of your bag that you've been practicing for weeks, then it's already over. Go home. Get a real job. It's over. You're not really dribbling. You're faking it.

If you really want to dribble, then the ball is not really in your hand. You are not where you are standing right now. You're not just one step ahead. That's kiddie shit. You're three ahead. You're three hundred ahead. You're three million ahead. You're gone. You *been* gone. The play is already over, and your team already scored the bucket, because the whole sequence happened in your imagination a half-second ago. As a point guard, you have to exist in another heavenly realm.

If you're laughing, *I'm* laughing. But the joke ain't on me, son.

Dribbling is spiritual. Facts.

Now, I didn't know *any* of this the first time I picked up a basketball. I just felt that worn leather in my hands, and it was awkward. It's not like I was born with any special gift. I started playing ball at the park after school, and during those first few months my dumb ass was just trying to do stupid tricks—doing the crab dribble, putting the ball around my back and all that. I wasn't really playing *basketball* basketball. I definitely wasn't dribbling. I was just messing around, trying to entertain people like the dudes I saw at the Rucker.

Yo, remember earlier, when I was telling you that a best friend can change your life? The same goes for a great teacher. And my teachers? My teachers wasn't just no ordinary teachers. If you're sensing a pattern in our little story here, then you better get used to it.

When I was thirteen, I had this PE teacher who kept giving me hell for the way I played basketball. His name was Mr. Archibald. Unassuming dude. Real cool. He wasn't in bad shape either. Now at that point, I had started making a little bit of a name for myself playing in the streets. So I would be in gym class doing all these crazy tricks for my friends, and it used to piss this PE teacher off so bad. He was old-school. He was trying to teach me how to do a crisp bounce pass or whatever, but I wasn't hearing it.

So this particular day, he's lecturing me, like, "Son, you don't know anything about *real* basketball. Get out of here with all these tricks."

Of course, I'm young and arrogant. So I turn around and I say, "*What*, old man? You don't know what you're talking about. You're just a bum-ass gym teacher."

Everybody's like, *Ooooohhhhhhhhh!*

I get in trouble, of course. Report to the principal's office. Whatever. A couple of weeks pass, and I get my hands on this VHS tape called *Below the Rim*. I don't even know how I got it. One of my boys must have left it at my house, because I definitely didn't have money for no VHS tape. It was like a mixtape of all the best NBA guards—Kevin Johnson, Jason Kidd, Isiah Thomas. I had never watched fifteen minutes of the NBA in my life up to that point. I'm watching this grainy-ass tape on an old-ass VCR that I copped from my uncle, and it's like my introduction to the league. It's a history lesson. Then in the middle of the tape they had this section for all the OG point guards from the '70s. I'm talking like Pistol Pete Maravich, Earl "the Pearl" Monroe, Oscar Robinson, Clyde Frazier—all these legends I've never heard of.

So I'm sitting there in front of the TV, eating my chicken nuggets or whatever, and all of a sudden they show this dude named Nate "Tiny" Archibald. The tube socks. The Converse hi-tops. The short shorts. He's kinda *nice.*

And I'm like, "Wait a minute. Hold up. Nah . . . *nahhhh.*"

I rewind the tape.

I'm like, "That dude look just like . . . *nahhhh, son!*"

I rewind the tape like twenty times.

Finally, I'm like, "Yo, this dude looks *just* like my PE teacher."

Mannnn, I go to gym class the next day and I'm looking at Mr. Archibald for the whole period like . . . *Is* it him? Nah, man. There's no *way.*

I'm squinting. I'm scrutinizing his hairline. I'm watching the way this man walks. I'm looking at his shoes, like: Yo, *if Mr. Archibald got NBA money, why is he wearing them old shoes?*

I start beating around the bush, asking him questions like: "Hey Mr. Archibald, what kind of car you drive?"

This man is taking the *subway* here? This ain't Tiny Archibald, man. But he looks *just* like the guy on the tape.

Finally, I can't take it anymore. I work up the courage to go up to him, and I'm like, "Hey, Mr. Archibald, do you have a son named Tiny Archibald?"

"No."

"Nah? For real? Mr. Archibald, this is crazy but you look just like this dude on my tape who plays for the Celtics?"

And all he says is, "Yeah. That's me."

Just like that. No smile. No ego.

And I'm losing my mind. I'm pointing at him like, "Man, you're TINY ARCHIBALD? You're on my VHS tape! Why didn't you *say* something?!"

Mr. Archibald is looking at me real calm, like Yoda.

He's like, "You ready to listen to me now?"

I'm like, "*Hell yeah*. Show me the way."

I mean—for all the young kids out there who don't understand—this is really like the equivalent of you acting up in your eighth-grade gym class, and the next day you go up to your teacher like, "*Yo, Mr. Paul!!! Are you really* Chris Paul, *man?*"

And Mr. Paul is rocking some khakis and a polo and he's like, "Yeah. I'm him."

I know it sounds fake. But that's really a true story. My friends were all Top 50 all-time rappers. What you think my gym teacher's gonna be? Top 50. It's providence.

From that day on, Tiny Archibald changed my life. He was the one who told me to focus on my handle, because in his infinite wisdom, he said, "If you can dribble, you'll always have a job."

He was the one who was telling me that I could go to college to play ball, and they would actually *pay* for it.

I said, "I can go to college for free? And my momma don't have to pay nothing?"

Mr. Archibald said, "For free. These days, you might even get you some free sneakers too. Y'all kids got it made now. Back in my day . . ."

"Aight, Mr. Archibald. Whatever, bro." (Now I'm Mr. Archibald. Funny how time flies.)

From that moment on, I probably dribbled six hours a day—no exaggeration. I'd take the ball everywhere. If I was on the subway, it was with me. If I was walking to school, I had a ball. If we went to get Chinese food, I'm eating a chicken wing with one hand and dribbling with the other. It was like an extension of my body. I would obsess over little ways that I could get better. When I used to watch my father train boxers when I was a little kid, he used to make them shadowbox with ankle weights strapped to their wrists to make their hands faster. I didn't have any trainers or coaches, so I had to get creative. I thought, *Yo, maybe if I strap some weights to my wrist while I dribble, I'll get quicker.*

It was nuts, but it worked. Now my hands are so quick that I don't even have to think about them anymore. I'm *one* with the ball. It's like I can feel it so well that I don't even feel it. It's not there. So now I'm dribbling without any fear. I'm dribbling wide and *loose* and free. Back then, everybody dribbled "inside the box." Nice and tight, like Kevin Johnson and Isiah Thomas. But when I started training with the wrist weights, all of a sudden the width of my dribble got super wide and super quick. Without even knowing what I was doing, I was inventing a new kind of street style. I'm not saying I invented the crossover. But I was part of a generation who invented it.

It got to the point where I was so comfortable and so fast that my hands were simply an illusion. I'm playing three-card monte with 'em now. You can't swipe me. It's already too late. Now you see it, now you don't.

Everything happened really fast. After about six months of working every day, I leveled up. Now I'm on phase 2. Now I'm dribbling with my *mind*. I'm *floating*. I'm like a bird. I'm *above* the court, and I can see the whole picture. Now we're playing mental chess. Every space, every pawn on the board, I am manipulating it with my mind. Remember that VHS tape I told you about? I used to get up in the morning before everybody was awake and watch the tape in slow motion. Pause. Rewind. Pause. Rewind. I started realizing what these guys were doing with their feet. It's just like watching a ballerina. When you watch a ballet, where do your eyes go? What are you looking at?

You're watching from the *toes up*.

It's the exact same thing with ball players.

The feet are the secret. The eyes, the shoulders, the hands, a quick little raise of the *eyebrow*—that's all just part of the illusion. That's the hustle. That's the magic trick. The feet are the real secret.

I used to go play 21 during the day, and in Harlem when you're playing 21, it's not four or five dudes playing. When you get the ball, it's one-on-fifteen. You're playing against grown-ass men. It's the Royal Rumble. You need to be so creative just to survive and find some space to get a shot up. I'd play for four, five hours against real dudes. Then at night, when everybody left for the burger spot or the house party, I'd play 21 in my mind versus an army of imaginary defenders. It got to the point where I could see them so vividly that it was no different from playing against real people.

But the thing is, I am not the hero in my imagination, you feel me? I am not Michael Jordan. I don't have superpowers. In my imagination, these defenders are *monsters*. They're seven feet tall, they're faster than me, and they're *talking shit*. They're all over me. Pressuring me. Suffocating me. I gotta use every last fiber in my body just to get a shot off. I'm sweating through my shirt. I'm falling down on the pavement getting bloody knees. I'm talking shit back to them, in my head: "Fuck you then! Fuck you, son! You ain't shit! *I'm* the man around here, son."

But it's just me out there, all alone. The only sound you hear is the ball bouncing off the pavement and me breathing real heavy, like a boxer. You know that sound?

"Hahh! Hahh! *Hahh! Psheww! Pheww! Foooo!*"

I'd show up to the park the next day and I'd be embarrassing dudes, and they'd be like, "Damn, Shamm, where the hell you learn that move?"

I'd say, "I used it on you last night."

They didn't know what the hell I was talking about. Once I started dribbling, I never stopped. Even when I wasn't at the court, I was someplace else in my mind, on a court that never closed.

I remember teachers at school and even my friends' moms saying stuff like, "It's like Shamm is *with* y'all, but he's *not* with y'all. He's off in the clouds."

I thought about dribbling on a spiritual level. See, like I told you: Dribbling is not about basketball. It's about being comfortable in uncomfortable situations. It is about adjusting. It's about rolling with anything. It's about imagining where you want to go, and creating that future in your mind—and then willing that shit into existence. It's not about basketball. It's about *life*.

There were so many times when Cam and Mase and Woods and Pretty Boy Mike and Big L and all my homeboys would be walking past the park on the way to some block party like, "Yo! Shamm! You coming?"

And I'd be like, "Nah, I'll catch y'all later."

I was in my lab, creating. They'd be coming *back* from the party at two o'clock in the morning, and I'd still be out there pounding that pavement—*doot, doot, doot, dat-dat-doot, dat-dat-doot.*

The rhythm of the streets.

A lot of the time, I wouldn't even shoot the ball. I wouldn't let myself have that pleasure. I'd just dribble in one spot, relentlessly. I was like Nutso in *Above the Rim*. Out there by myself. Just me and the rats, bro. I remember there was this one particular streetlamp—it was the *good* streetlamp. Old reliable. When the other lights burned out, this one was always going strong. For some reason, the light used to cast my shadow perfectly on the pavement. It was so crisp. When I was all alone, that was my defender. My *nemesis.*

The summer before high school started, I got so nice that I was convinced that I was literally going to shake my own shadow. I'm not exaggerating. When I say I believed I could do it, I *believed* it. I probably spent like ten thousand hours just trying to cross up my shadow in the park.

That was the birth of "The Shammgod" that you hear about so much now. It wasn't at Providence College. It wasn't in the Big East tournament. The Shammgod was born in the streets. It wasn't a move. It was a mentality.

To me, dribbling was freedom. Freedom from fear. Freedom from poverty. Freedom from violence. Freedom from everything that was going on in my house at the time. Basketball took the pain away. Nobody is shooting. Nobody is fighting. Nobody is telling me what to do. See, I didn't have a father or an uncle or a coach telling me how to play the "right way." It was all in my head—ultimate freedom. I'm not doing it to get followers or to get a Bentley. I'm doing it for the love of it. I'd go home so late at night that the house would usually be peaceful. Everybody would be passed out asleep. I'd take a shower if the hot water was on, crash in bed, and start all over again the next day.

Looking back, I was so naive it was crazy. They say ignorance is bliss, but I'm surprised it didn't get my ass killed. When I had the ball in my hand, I had absolutely no fear. I had no awareness of anything or anyone. It was like time ceased to exist. I ceased to exist. So I would be playing pickup at 145th Street Park against drug dealers, real gangsters, I'm talking about *real known killers*, and I'd be talking *wild nonsense* to these guys. I'm *fourteen*, son. I weigh like 120 pounds, and I'm talking to grown men with bodies on them like, "You think you good, huh? You ain't shit. Get this man outta here. He can't guard me."

One time we were playing a tournament over in West Harlem, one of those side games for a little money, and I dribbled the ball between the defender's legs, and as I did it, I don't know what came over me, but I pulled homeboy's shorts down. The whole gym went crazy.

Ten minutes later, when the game is over, me and my whole team are running for our lives. We're sprinting out of the gym and down the block with a bunch of gangsters chasing us. And my teammates are looking at me like, "You really had to do that, huh? *Really, bro?*"

This one day, I vividly remember talking shit to this guy, and I came off the court and Mase went white as a ghost. He pulls me aside like, "Yo, Shamm, chill. You know who that is, right?"

I'm like, "He ain't nobody."

He's like, "Bro, do you know what he does for a living?"

"He ain't shit. He work at McDonald's."

"Bro, he's a hit man. This ain't a movie. He really a *hit man*."

Mannnnn, I went and dapped homeboy up like, "Yo, good game, good game, good game. It's all love, big homie. Y'all played hard."

Hahahahah. Facts. Dude was probably already telling his boys where to bury my body. But that's just how I was, when I was playing ball. Nothing else mattered.

That was just the cost of doing business in the hood. If you were playing ball, you were probably playing against some gangsters. That man across from you might have bodies on him, but you couldn't think about it. You couldn't be scared; otherwise you'd never leave your damn house in the morning.

One of the first lessons you learn early on in the hood is that you need to be very careful who you say are the good guys and who you say are the villains. At times, when my father got locked up, there were drug dealers who were paying my mother's rent when she was too sick to get on her own two feet. Because of who my father was in the streets and the stature he had in the Black Panthers community, they looked out for us. They kept us from getting evicted. They kept food on our table. And not just me, but a lot of families. I've seen drug dealers take fifteen blocks of people in the projects to the Six Flags in New Jersey—buses, tickets, food, everything paid for. Real gangsters put new Nikes on my feet just because I had a good game at the park. They never asked me for anything in return. They just respected me. They knew that I could be something. Are they the villains? Are they the good guys? It depends which way you're looking at it. But when you're a kid growing up in the hood, you don't have the luxury of looking at it through the lens of morality. Leave the morality for the college professors. We're about *reality*. You fuck with me? Then I fuck with you. How you make your money ain't none of my business. We not out here comparing W-2s. We're just trying to eat.

Prime example: One of the first people in Harlem who really put me on was this guy named "KC." He was actually the first dude I met when we moved to Harlem, even before I started going to school and I met Mase. My "godbrother" Stormin' Norman, a family friend, took me to this store on 125th right across from the Apollo called BOSS Emporium. I've never seen anything like it in my life, even to this day. You remember FAO Schwarz, the toy store from *Home Alone 2* with the big fifty-foot toy in the middle of the store? BOSS was the hood version of FAO Schwarz. It didn't seem real. This was some Willy Wonka shit, street fashion.

I walk in and there's a brand-new BMW sitting in the middle of the store. Custom interior. Chrome BBS wheels. Looks like it's never even been driven. It's just there on display. On all the racks, I'm seeing the flyest clothes. What now I guess they're calling "streetwear" and selling for $600 a T-shirt, BOSS was selling all that stuff damn near thirty-five years ago. Stacks of those orange Nike boxes on every wall. I had never even seen Nikes in real life in Crown Heights. They got the big speakers playing Big Daddy Kane. Not the Casio boom box, son. I'm talking *speakers*. I never heard *bass* like that before. Bumpin', *thumpin'* your chest. The entire store was designed to look like a street corner. So you could be out on the corner with your homeboys even when it was raining. They even had a real pay phone in there with the glass booth and everything. If you ever had no money in your pocket and you had to call your momma, you could run into BOSS and use the pay phone for free. Mind you, I'm ten years old at this point. I'm looking up at Stormin' Norman like, *Yo, where are we right now? Who owns all this?*

Right on cue, out the back of the store walks KC. You know how in the movies when a bad motherfucker gets introduced to the story, and the camera goes super-slow-motion, and homeboy walks through the door with a real swagger, like he owns the joint?

Well, picture that. Because this motherfucker owned the joint. KC was the King of 125th Street.

He got the wavy hair. He got the freshest sneakers. He's rocking the red Reebok 5411 hi-tops with the double Velcro. He got the Champion tracksuit. Gold chain. He's young, successful, and the whole place smells like *money*. And most importantly, he's got something more important than money. He's got the knowledge. The minute he starts talking to me I'm like: *Oh, this dude is* smart *smart*.

People telling me, "You know what young money got on his SATs? He broke the damn machine. It ain't know how to count that high."

From the jump, KC took a liking to me for some reason. Maybe because I was quiet and observant like him. He took me under his wing and started schooling a lost Brooklyn kid on what it meant to be *Harlem*. Where to go, where not to go, who to talk to, how to move in the streets, who to call if somebody is giving your mom any trouble. He never raised his voice. It was always super calm and steady. Dude is wearing a $5,000 watch, and every time I see him, all he wants to talk about is, "How you like school? What you learning about? You like history? You need to know your history. I want to see you bringing straight As in here. You bring in some As, and I might have a little something for you."

Everybody else wanted to talk about who's better—Big Daddy Kane or Rakim. KC wanted to talk about Malcolm X and Marcus Garvey and what we were learning in math class. He was just *different*. God was showing me a different path.

Early on, with my father in jail, KC and Stormin' Norman kept my head above water. They were like my cool older brothers or uncles who always knew the answer to any question. A few years later, when I started playing organized ball, KC would sponsor these teams and take us to play in tournaments outside of New York. Money games, we called them. Don't think AAU or travel basketball. We're off the books, you feel me? It was the first time I ever left the city. We'd hop in a bunch of SUVs and he and his boys would drive us there, pay for the hotels, pay for the food— no questions asked. We'd be down in North Carolina, and it was the first time I was smelling that country air. That crispy pine tree air. Real darkness. No neon. No sirens. It was the first time I was really seeing all the stars in the sky at night. I remember me and my boys looking up like, "Dang, I only ever seen stars like this in the *movies*, B."

Every time I left the city, it was like a little breather from all the pressure of being the man of the house. But at the same time, I used to have a lot of anxiety leaving my mom alone back in Harlem.

She was struggling a lot at that time, drinking way too much, and I remember I used to call her from some Motel 6 somewhere and she'd be like, "Where you at? I haven't seen you in two days."

"I'm in North Carolina playing basketball, Mom."

"North *Carolina*?"

"Yeah, don't worry about it, Ma. KC got us."

I didn't ask any questions about where the money was coming from. I mean, I'm twelve, thirteen years old. I'm just seeing a young black man with his own clothing store, his own record label, driving around a new car like a boss in the streets, and it was inspiring to me. He's got two babies at home, and he's taking care of fifteen to twenty kids in the neighborhood, just making sure they got something to eat and they don't got holes in their socks.

Years later, I am sitting in my dorm room during my freshman year of college, and I'm surfing channels. I'm half-asleep. I'm dozing off. And I got on *America's Most Wanted*. They're talking about this dude who was moving kilos. Moving kilos in Harlem. Now I perk up a little bit. I probably know this guy. Who they talking about? [Redacted] from around the way? [Redacted] who was doing business with the Medellín cartel?

Nah.

I see the picture.

"[Redacted]. Also known as KC. One of New York's biggest kingpins."

I almost fell out of the bed. I called up my mans back home like, "Yo! Turn on the TV! Are you seeing this? They got KC on the TV."

You have to understand, this man moved so quietly. He was the antigangster. These were the days of Rich Porter and Alpo. These were the days when drug dealers used to be paying rappers $500 just to shout out their name on a mixtape. KC wasn't out in the streets like that. He didn't go to parties. He had legitimate businesses. He wasn't a gangster. But he was a mastermind.

And he saved my life. Without KC Childs, you have never heard of me. I never make it to the NBA. I never even make it out the hood. To this day, he's one of my best friends in the world.

So I ask you once again: Is he a hero? A villain? Something in between?

KC and Stormin' Norman kept driving us around on the weekends to play the nicest crews from hoods all over America. And I kept getting better and better. Around that time, when I was maybe thirteen, I stopped being "Dudley" and my name started ringing out as "Shammgod, Shammgod, Shammgod."

Very slowly, the streets were taking notice.

"You seen what Shammgod did the other day? That boy Shammgod *nice*."

The next summer, when I was around fourteen, I got introduced to this dude Thurman Player, who ran the basketball team for this Christian organization called Young Life. He was getting kids together from all over the city to play for his team, and it was like the Avengers. The baddest dudes from Harlem, Bed-Stuy, Queens, Coney Island. I show up to Salem Church one day, and I'm meeting this kid named Stephon Marbury, straight out of Coney Island. I'm meeting this kid outta Jamaica, Queens, named Rafer Alston (aka "Skip 2 My Lou"), I'm meeting this kid outta the Bronx named Kareem Reid. And I bring along my boy from Harlem, Tyrone Evans (aka "Alimoe," aka "Black Widow").

If you know, *you know*. We're talking about five of the most devastating dudes to ever handle that rock, all standing together in a church basement in Staten Island. All of us just kids. All of us broke as a joke. All of us hungry as hell to make it out. Young Life wasn't exactly AAU either, but it was my first introduction to real organized basketball. And there was real money floating around it. What today they got all the lawyers and the PR people calling NIL (name, image, and likeness) money. We just called it some handshake money. You win a tournament with Young Life? You might get your momma's electric bill paid. Take you a hot shower. You play really good? Might get you a Starter jacket. As long as you were balling, you didn't have to be sweeping the floors at the West Indian spot, you feel me?

Everybody wanted to be a star. Everybody wanted to be that one kid in ten thousand that made it out.

I remember at some point somebody saying, "Yo, so which one of us is gonna play *point guard*?"

Five hands went straight up. And New York City being New York City, those hands *stayed up*.

"Yo, you Bronx dudes can't dribble. Come on, son. Y'all can't even tie your shoelaces."

"Nah! Nah, dunny. *I* want the rock. You set the picks, B."

"We ain't setting no picks. Y'all just clear out for *me*. Show you how we do it in Coney *Eye-land*, son."

Finally, somebody pointed to Steph and they're like: "Yo, do you know who that is? That's Stephon Marbury. He's the number one ninth grader in the country."

I'm like, "The *country*? What're you talking the *country*?"

He said, "The *country*, B."

I said, "They got *rankings* for that? For *basketball*? Who even putting that out, the *United Nations*?"

He said, "He a bad motherfucker, B. He's number one."

I said, "Number one, huh? Alright . . . He can take the ball up."

I'm looking at Steph like: *Pssshhh. You ain't shit.*

He's looking at me like: *Oh, you about to see.*

I had no clue all the places we were about to go together. No clue that I was looking at one of the best point guards of all time. No clue that I was staring at my brother from another mother.

Steph. Shammgod. Skip. Alimoe. Kareem Reid. Real ones know.

Avengers, assemble. Let's get up out the hood.

You ever had a near-death experience? It's not like the movies. There's never any buildup. There's no soundtrack. There's no Hans Zimmer in the hood, you feel me? You never even see it coming. It just *happens*. Out of the blue, somebody pulls out a gun. And that gun is real. And that gun is pointing at *you*, son. You got just enough time to think to yourself: *Dang, this might be it, huh? Just like that?* It's so ridiculous that you almost want to laugh.

I almost died twice before the age of sixteen. The first time I ever had a gun put to my head, I was thirteen years old. It was the summertime, and in the summer, we used to be playing Manhunt all over the city. If you never played Manhunt as a kid, it's kind of like a combination of tag and hide-and-seek with two teams. If you get tagged, you gotta go to "jail" and then your homeboys can try to get around the guards and break you out of jail. Now, if you're from the suburbs, you're probably playing in a backyard or maybe a park or something. Little Jimmy is hiding under the swingset. Everybody goes home when the streetlights turn on. That's *soft*. This was a whole different thing.

In Harlem, the whole neighborhood was our territory. As soon as it got dark, somebody would scream out, "Manhunt!" and fifty kids would go running in every direction. It was *wild*. Nothing was off-limits. You'd really be hiding in the bodega behind stacks of beer cases, you feel me? You'd be looking at that bodega cat like, *Yo, don't be purring! They're coming! You're gonna blow up my spot!* We were in and out of buildings. You'd be chasing somebody through the *hospital wing*, B. Going up and down elevators, running through the subway, hopping the turnstiles. It's eleven o' clock at night, and you'd be sprinting through the Delanor Projects, telling the corner boys, "Ay, tell 'em I went the *other* way!"

The best part of those times was that you didn't have to spend any money to have fun. You'd be laughing till you cried, and it was all free. You'd go to the park after Manhunt, and everybody would regroup and hang out and share some Chinese food until one o' clock in the morning. Six chicken wings and a fried rice for $2.50. Sharing the 25-cent grape drink between four of your homeboys. Just shooting the shit, talking about who's the best rapper, who's the best ball player, who's the fliest shorty. No parental supervision required. They'd probably put you in jail for that these days, but these were *different days*. My mom had enough on her plate to deal with. At that point in time, she was drinking every night. To me, that was normal. The malt liquor, the shouting, the bottles smashing, the "tussling." Normal. A fish in water don't know he's in water. Now you'd call it domestic violence. Now the neighbors would be calling up

Child Services. But to me, and to a lot of us kids in Harlem at that time, it was just normal everyday life. Or maybe a better word for it is *raw*. If I call it normal, I'd be normalizing a fucked-up situation. But on the other hand, if I sugarcoat it for you and tell you that I was crying into my pillow every night, thinking that I was different, thinking that I had it harder than the kids I was growing up with . . . man, I'd just be bullshitting you. So let's just say it was *rawest* life you can imagine. To this day, the reason that I never drink or smoke is because of the way my mother and stepfather used to just be a slave to those vices. I remember my mom used to send me to the corner store to get her a pack of Newport 100s and her Colt 45s. I can still *smell* it, and I start hearing the opening bars to *General Hospital*. My mom loved that show. I'd be coming back from the store with her cigarettes, and she'd always be watching that soap, and of course I'm rolling my eyes like, "Yo, this is so stupid. Why do you care about Luke and Laura so much?"

And then gradually they're just reeling my ass in, day after day.

I'm coming home and sitting on the arm of the sofa, real curious, like, "Yo, what's up with shorty now? Why she crying?"

And my mom would fill me in on what was going down.

Then I'm coming home the next week, and now I'm sitting down on the cushions next to her like, "Damn, what did this crazy-ass white boy do now? Yo, he did *what*? Homeboy faked his own death? Yo!"

My mom is shushing me, like, "Quiet! Wait till the commercials!"

I was hooked, man. Shout-out to Luke and Laura. The whole hood was rooting for y'all.

I'm being funny, but that time with my mom was really special to me. Me and her watching her soaps, before I left to go play basketball, and before my stepfather got home from work, that was like the little calm in the storm for us. In a couple hours, when it got darker and the bottles started to pile up on the countertops, and my stepfather got home, and the music started to get loud, it might be a good night. But it might be a bad night. Or it might even be one of *them* nights. When the screaming starts, and I gotta grab a knife, or a hammer, and I gotta keep my ear to the bedroom door. When I gotta be ready to die.

If I smell that Newport 100 smoke to this very day, it all comes back to me, and I get a chill down my spine.

But see, this is where it gets complicated. Because when it comes to my stepfather, if you're looking for a pure villain in my story, you need to look elsewhere. I might've been ready to kill this dude some nights in order to protect my mother, but at the same time, he was the one that was getting up at five o'clock in the morning, working odd jobs just to put food on our table. He had major issues with anger. But the dude was *there*. He was the only male figure in my life at that time who was trying to provide for us. So my feelings for him, even now, are extremely complicated. It would probably take me twenty years in therapy to truly understand this motherfucker. And you have to remember, I was just thirteen years old when this was all going down, so as far as I was concerned, when it came to him and my mother's relationship, that was grown-folks business.

Every second I was out of our apartment and at the park with a basketball in my hands, I was *winning*. What my mother didn't know, she didn't *need* to know, you feel me? Now they're putting AirTags on these little motherfuckers. Moms be tracking these kids with drones. Me, back then? I'd be gone for *days* sometimes. "Where Shamm at? He at a sleepover?" Nah, I'm in the *Bronx*, Ma. I'm playing dice in the alleyway with OGs. I was just happy to stay out on the streets and away from the chaos in my house for as long as possible. I know pearls are being clutched right now all over America as I'm telling you this, but the honest truth is, most of the time, if you're minding your own business, the streets have a way of looking out for you. If you're a stand-up dude, you're not going to have any problems.

Most of the time. But not every time. That's the thing about the hood. It only takes one moment for things to go bad. It only takes somebody having a bad day, and before you know it, you're staring down the barrel of a gun. That's what happened to me the summer after I turned thirteen. We had just come back from the park after Manhunt. Me, Zig, Woods, Howie, Pretty Boy Mike, and a bunch of kids. We used to always sit on this railing outside this apartment building on 143rd Street. That's what you do when you got no money in the summer of 1989 in Harlem. You sit on a railing and talk. You're posted up for three hours with your boys, taking in the view of the next project building, just people watching. That wasn't just any railing, that was *our* railing, you understand?

So we were posted up, talking about "Nah, *Rakim* is the best rapper . . . Nah—" when this random dude walks up the steps with his girl. And she was fly. Everybody who ever grew up in the hood just had a shiver go down their spine. I guarantee it. You already know where this shit is going, don't you? You can hear the horror-movie music, right? See, people outside the hood, they think a dangerous situation in Harlem is walking down a dark alley at two o'clock in the morning. No, bro. The most dangerous situation in the world is three teenagers chilling on a stoop or a railing or outside a corner store when a random dude walks up with his girl, and his girl got that *thang* on her.

You already know what is about to happen. Shit is about to go bad, real quick. But for the people outside the hood, what happened was this:

My boy said, "Oooohhhhhh *shit*."

He said it in a way that only a thirteen-year-old kid from Harlem can say it.

He turned to us with the *Looney Tunes* expression. His eyeballs were coming out his damn skull. He was Daffy Duckin'.

He said, "Yoooooo! She got a *big* ol' booty!"

Now, he said this in a positive way. That's what you need to understand. He said this with so much admiration. So much respect. I can't think of a higher degree of respect you could give in that situation. What he meant was "Sir, I tip my hat to you. Miss, I bow down to you. Tonight, you have truly blessed us. Thank you."

But at one o'clock in the morning in Harlem, that was not how homeboy took it.

When the dude turned around, I happened to be the closest one to him. That's when the gun came out. He put it right up to my head. That's an interesting sensation, feeling the chrome on your forehead. Feeling the weight of it—how *real* it all is. You don't really have time to think or to explain anything. Life doesn't flash before your eyes. It almost seems like a joke.

He said, "Oh, you think it's funny? Well, this is what *I* think is funny. I'm gonna kill you. Ain't that funny?"

I didn't even know what to say. I just looked at him, like: *Nah, it's not funny, B. Just let me go home.* And I remember he said, "I'll end your life *right now.*"

I'll never forget that moment, because he was definitely a killer. You know when you're talking to a real killer. That's something you can't fake. He was serious. A couple of centimeters— a little squeeze of a finger, and my life would have been over at fourteen. Dead over nothing. Over something my friend said to make everybody laugh. I would've been another sob story. But in that moment, I can vividly remember feeling this weird sensation come over my body. It wasn't fear. It was the opposite of fear. I was looking at this gun, and I just had this certainty that it wasn't my time to go yet. That this was not my ending. I had too much left to do in life. It was like I could feel God protecting me with this *aura*, the same way he was protecting me from my stepfather when he was having one of those bad nights. The same way he protected me when I was sleeping alone on the bench in the alleyway. But there was a flip side to that coin. It was like we made an understanding, in those moments. See, it was like I owed God a *debt*. He was keeping me around so that I could go on to do something bigger—bigger than basketball, bigger than Harlem, bigger even than my own life. When God speaks to you like that, it doesn't come as words that I can repeat back to you. It's deeper than that. It's this sensation that you feel in your *soul*, you got me? And in that moment, with a gun to my head, I understood everything.

I looked the dude in the eyes, like: *We don't gotta do this, homie. Let's all just go home.* And he lowered the gun. Everybody exhaled. He put it in his back pocket and turned around. Him and his girl went inside.

But because this was Harlem, the last thing he said was "Don't worry if she got a big booty or not."

My boys were looking at me wide-eyed, scared to death. I just shrugged my shoulders and said, "Yo, don't worry about it. I thought it was a *compliment*."

The second time I almost died was scarier. The second time, I didn't hear God speaking to me. The second time . . . I really thought that it was a wrap. Now, I know I told you that I wasn't in the streets. And that's not a lie. Not exactly. But it's more like a half-truth. See, I wasn't *in* the streets. But I was *of* the streets. You follow me? I mean, by the time I'm thirteen, fourteen, fifteen years old, the early-'90s crack era is in full swing. This is not the Run-DMC Era anymore. This is not MC Hammer and parachute pants. This is not the era of smoking reefer with the bamboo paper and drinking St. Ides. That was old-folks shit. This is the N.W.A era now. This is Biggie and Pac. This is crack rock or jump shots. And why would you even want to play ball anyway? Jordan is only making $3 million a year, sweating his ass off. Crack dealers were making $5 million for standing around on the corner. Big money was flowing in to the hustlers in every borough, but everybody was *taking* that money and showing it off in Harlem. We were the epicenter. And that's when things really started popping off. That's when people started dying every day. That's when you couldn't even trust your own people anymore. That's when you had to be in a little crew just for protection, whether you wanted to be in the game or you wanted to go to the library. That's when they started getting ruthless. That's when they started kidnapping children straight off the school bus.

If you have ever seen the movie *Paid in Full*, then you know the story of Donnell Porter. But it wasn't fiction to us. It was a documentary. I *knew* Donnell. He went to my school. He was two years younger than me. His older brother was Rich Porter, who had a little empire going in Harlem at that time with his partner Alpo. Even if you're not from the hood, you've heard those names ring out in rap songs for the last twenty years. And for good reason. Rich Porter and Alpo were kings. They ran the city. That's not hyperbole. *Paid in Full* was probably the only gangster movie ever made that was *too* subtle. They made Rich and Alpo into run-of-the-mill gangsters. But they were so wild and flamboyant in real life that it would've been unfilmable. People wouldn't have believed how they moved through the city. Alpo used to be popping wheelies on Japanese superbikes on the Brooklyn Bridge, wearing a four-thousand-dollar mink coat. He was like an anime character, B. The original antihero. He'd be pulling up to Willie Burger at three o'clock in the morning in the C300 with the Louis Vuitton duffel bag, buying out the whole spot.

Oh, you don't know about Willie Burger? Then you're not from New York City, son. For the uninitiated, there was this famous burger spot on 145th and Eighth Avenue called Willie's Burgers, aka *Willie Burger*, aka *Yo we goin' to Willie*. This was the spot. This was the club that wasn't a club. The club that was open to everybody, 24/7. Food better than your grandma makes. The handwritten sign pasted up on the front of the stand from the 1960s: Sweet Potato Pie. Spicy Jumbo Turkey Burger. Fresh Fish Chips. Jalapeno Burger. Italian Burger. Arepas.

You could get anything at Willie Burger. Homegirl behind the grill would've probably made you a whole Thanksgiving turkey if you paid cash. Willie Burger was *America*, B. Willie Burger was *democracy*. You could be wearing your ball shorts and a sweaty T-shirt and still go chill in the parking lot of Willie's and try to holler at the girls coming back from the club in Balenciaga. You hang around looking hungry enough and eventually somebody would pull up in a Porsche and buy you and all your homeboys a turkey burger. Rich Porter and Alpo used to pull up all the time. AZ. Jay-Z. Fat Joe. Puff. LL Cool J. You'd see Dame Dash shooting dice in the parking lot on the hood of a BMW that only came out in Germany. *Facts*. Today, these kids are talking about "these Jordans ain't even out yet. Got 'em off the *internet*." That's soft. Back in the day, motherfuckers were making so much money they had cars coming in from *Dusseldorf*. They had international freight under their control. They were moving whips across the Atlantic. Rich Porter would pull up to Willie Burger in an Aston Martin sitting on the *other side* of the whip. That's a flex. When your car is so rare the wheel is on the right side. "Yo, this shit is only out in *London*." So don't tell me about your Jordans, son. These guys were on another level.

Me and Mase used to go there after playing ball in the park just so Mase could start freestyling in front of everybody and try to make a name for himself. My dude used to love to argue with everybody about hip-hop. You know how many times I've seen Mase in an argument with Jay-Z or Fat Joe about who's the best rapper? This was before anybody was *anybody*. They were having the same exact arguments that people have now, in the parking lot of Willie Burger, sharing a basket of french fries and almost coming to blows over Big Daddy Kane versus 2Pac.

It got to the point that there were so many hustlers pulling up to Willie Burger on a Saturday night that the feds were planting agents in the crowd. People couldn't even trust their own family members. Once enough money starts to flow into anything— I don't care what it is—it gets to the point where people lose sight of God. They start doing things that would have seemed unthinkable before. Around that time, people started turning into rats for the feds. Once things get chaotic like that, the wolves come out.

That's when Donnell got kidnapped. He was literally walking to school one morning when a van pulled up, and he got snatched in broad daylight. The crew that took him sent a note demanding half a mil in cash from Rich. He didn't have enough cash on hand to pay the ransom, so the kidnappers told him to look for a reply in the bathroom of the McDonald's on 125th Street.

Rich's crew went to the McDonald's and found a coffee cup taped to the underside of the bathroom sink. Inside the cup was Donnell's pinky finger. There was a cassette tape in there too. It was a recording of Donnell begging for his life. Can you imagine that? A twelve-year-old kid. The rumors started going around school about what happened. Kids didn't even feel safe getting off the bus. Who are they gonna take next?

That's when everybody went to war. There was so much paranoia, and so much backstabbing going on. The feds had taps going on everybody. The walls were closing in on a lot of the big crews. That winter, things got super dark. Right after New Year's Day 1990, Rich Porter was found murdered. It was like the closing of a chapter in the golden era of Harlem. The only thing darker than Rich getting killed was when they found out who shot him. It was his own partner, his own homeboy. Alpo.

Shit was Shakespearean, B. And it wasn't over.

Three weeks later, they discovered Donnell's body chopped up in plastic bags on a bike path in the Bronx. I remember thinking: *Yo, who the fuck kidnaps a little boy and kills him over* money? It didn't sit right with me. There was all kinds of money floating around New York at that time. When something like that happens, it's always somebody close to you. It wasn't until years later that the feds found out who was behind the kidnapping. The streets knew first. It turned out to be Donnell's own uncle, Apple Porter.

This man had his own *blood* snatched up on the way to school. He murdered his own kin. All over greed. All over jealousy. That's why I tell people all the time—they always fail when they make movies about Harlem during that era. Because they are always trying to make everything too Hollywood. Our life wasn't Hollywood. It was biblical.

When Rich died, that was the start of the dark days. Whenever the generals get taken out or put behind bars, like what happened in 1990, that's when things get really unpredictable. You don't need to read *The Art of War* to know exactly what happens next. Once you have a power vacuum, there's no control anymore. The old ways die out. The kids start running the projects, and they don't have the same code of ethics. Innocent people start getting hurt. It becomes senseless. *Chaos.* That was the environment I was coming up in right before my freshman year of high school, when I had just got hooked up with Stephon Marbury and Skip and Ali-moe and the Avengers. Funny, right? Right when I saw the light at the end of the tunnel. Harlem was in the middle of a civil war.

Here's the thing about a war zone: There's no keeping your head down. There's no minding your own business. Have you ever heard that old saying about war? I don't know who said it, but it's true. "You might not be interested in war. But war is *definitely* interested in you." That was life in Harlem in 1989. Everybody knew somebody who was involved in the drug trade.

If it wasn't your cousin, it was your homeboy. As soon as you stepped outside your door, you were in the game whether you liked it or not. Basketball was my protective shield from a lot of it. If I had a basketball in my hand, I felt like I could be in any type of situation, and I could just start dribbling and be off in my own world. People would either leave me alone or they'd say, "Damn, son, let me see that move again!" It was a way of defusing any situation.

"Yo, I'm just over here with my ball. Leave me at peace, B."

But once high school rolled around, some of my boys started doing low-level stuff just to eat. It's hard to say no to that cash money when your momma is on welfare. When you got brothers and sisters telling you they're hungry. A lot of my boys were providers at fourteen years old. One of my best friends Zig, he ran the corner right next to the park where I'd practice every night. It was perfect because I could be out there until one o'clock in the morning doing my psychotic dribbling drills, trying to shake my shadow, and Zig would be across the way doing his little hand-to-hand business. If I saw anybody suspicious coming through the park, I'd give him a little whistle. Just a heads-up. I was what they call a lookout boy. Ninety-nine percent of the night, I was just dribbling under the streetlights, minding my own business. But if you were a cop walking through the park at one o'clock in the morning, I was gonna let my boy know. If you were part of another crew, and you weren't supposed to be on *our side* of the park, I was gonna let my boy know. That was the job. When his shift was over, we'd go to Willie Burger and Zig would buy all the food. Maybe he'd toss me forty bucks every once in a while. It was informal. That was just my boy, you know? So like I said: I wasn't really *in* the streets. But I was *of* the streets. And that was enough to get you killed in 1990.

I can remember this clear as day. I still have dreams about it sometimes. We were walking back from Willie Burger like we had done a million times before. It was two o'clock in the morning. Belly full. Feeling on top of the world. Talking about—what else?—who's the best rapper, who's the flyest chick—when out of nowhere, this car pulls up. There's a certain way that a car follows you in the hood that will send chills down your spine. It doesn't pull up in a friendly way, you feel me? It creeps. The windows are tinted. Can't see shit inside. It stops right beside you. *Damn. We got a problem.* The moment I saw both windows rolling down at the same time, that's when I *knew*. They're not asking for directions. *I'm dead.* I don't know why. I don't got any time to ask questions. I'm just dead. Before the windows even fully rolled down, my boy took off running. I was frozen. Then I saw the gun come out. Two guns. Three guns. And I took off running the other way. I dropped my basketball and everything.

And all I heard was . . .

Bop, bop, bop bop bop bop.

I didn't know if they were shooting at me or my boy. They got out of the car and started yelling.

Bop, bop, bop bop bop bop.

I could feel the wind from the bullets. They're shooting at me. I'm dead.

Bop bop bop bop.

I'm running for my life. Then I hear them get back in the car. Doors slam. Engine starts back up again. *Alright, I'm safe.* And then it was like a bad dream. I turned for a split second and I looked behind me. They threw the car in reverse, put the pedal to the metal, and they were driving down the alley after me.

That's when I realized I was running down a one-way street. I was looking for a store or an apartment building or an alleyway I could jump into. There was nothing. So I just kept running for my life. I could hear the engine getting closer and closer behind me, and I thought, *That's it. This is my time. I can't outrun a car. I'm gonna die tonight.*

I never looked back again. I was just waiting to feel the shots.

But for some reason . . . The car just zoomed right past me. I don't know if they realized that they had the wrong kid or if they were just worried about the cops coming, but they stopped shooting. They sped past me and got up out of there. I stopped running and I collapsed in the middle of the street.

There were a couple people on the block, and they were looking at me like they seen a *ghost.* Somebody said, "I thought they were gonna kill you, son."

All I could think was: *Yo, I got another chance. I'm reborn. Thank you, God.*

I ran to the park and found Zig.

I told him, "Find yourself a new lookout, son. Fuck this. I'm *done.*"

He said, "Come on, B. Relax. What you gonna do for money?"

I said, "What I'mma do? I'm gonna be a *ball player*."

He laughed. Everybody was always laughing at that.

Then I remembered something.

These motherfuckers made me drop my basketball.

I dropped it when I ran away. I was never getting that ball back. I had broken it in *perfect* too. I had worked that leather all over New York City. I knew every groove of that ball. It was an extension of me.

And I remember thinking, *Never again, B. Never again. If you wanna take the ball from me, you're gonna have to kill me first.*

5

We used to read these things called magazines. The internet, it's soft. Let's be real. People hiding behind a keyboard. *Soft.* Grown men tippy-tapping out gossip every day. *Soft.* I don't mess with it. Magazines, they were the real thing. They were *official*. The basketball magazines back in the '90s, it was like the gospel coming down from on high and telling you who was *really* nice. Now, I didn't know anything about these magazines until I got to high school. I was in my own little world. Stephon Marbury was my window into the wider basketball world. Real basketball, not streetball. Steph knew everything. He was cultured in a way that I wasn't, because he had a whole team around him—his older brothers, his cousins, his dad. They were a unit. I just had me, myself, and I. Once I started playing ball with Steph on our travel team and we got tight, he would invite me to come out to Coney Island and train with him and his brothers. These dudes would never shut up about Kenny Anderson.

I didn't even know who Kenny Anderson was at the time. I barely knew about Michael Jordan and Magic Johnson. Steph and his brothers were always talking about "*Kinny*Anderson, *Kinny*-Anderson. You see what *Kinny* did?"

Finally, I said, "Yo, who the hell is Kenny Anderson?"

"You don't know *Kinny* Anderson? Yo, is he serious? Where did you find this kid, Steph? He's wylin', son! For your information, *Kinny* Anderson is the man at Georgia Tech. He's from around the way in Queens. He's about to go to the NBA."

I'm like, "Yo, what the hell is Georgia Tech?"

I was so naive about the business of basketball. Nobody in my family went to college. I didn't know anything outside of New York. But Steph and his brothers took me to school. They started showing me VHS tapes of Kenny playing at Georgia Tech, and he was the smoothest dude I had ever seen on a basketball court. Everything he did was effortless. Him and the ball were one entity. Harmonious. It was beautiful. We used to watch the tape and then rewind it and watch it again. Then I started looking at Steph like, *Wait a minute. This motherfucker is walking exactly like Kenny Anderson. He's dribbling like Kenny Anderson. He even got the middle part in his fade like Kenny Anderson!* Literally, Steph used to actually *look in the mirror* and try to move like Kenny. Shrug his shoulders like Kenny. Chew gum like Kenny. That was his idol.

So of course I became obsessed with Kenny too. Me and Steph used to play one-on-one—Kenny Anderson versus *Kenny Anderson*. You know that Spider-Man meme? Spider-Man pointing at Spider-Man. That was us playing ball in the park at one o'clock in the morning in Coney Island. Who could be the *most Kenny*.

We'd be out there on the blacktop drenched in sweat, sitting on top of the basketball after we were done playing, just dreaming, like . . .

"Yo, in four years, I'm gonna be at Georgia Tech, killing it."

"Yo, in four years, *I'm* gonna be at Georgia Tech, *killing it.* You can be the shooting guard, son."

"Wonder how the shorties are out there . . ."

"I heard they're *nice,* B."

I didn't even know what city Georgia Tech was in. To me, it was just some amazing place that existed only in my mind, like paradise.

We'd go back to Steph's apartment, and his brothers were always reading this magazine called *Hoop Scoop.* It was this little independent thing, nothing fancy. Almost like the pamphlets you'd get at church. I don't even know how they went about it, or what the methodology was, but they used to rank all the high school players in New York City and print it in the magazine at the end of the year. Now, you gotta understand how different me and Steph were at that point in time, at the start of high school. I went to La Salle Academy in Lower Manhattan. Catholic school. All boys. Uniforms. Button-ups and khakis every day. Steph went to Abraham Lincoln High School in Coney Island. We just played together on our AAU travel team on the weekends, doing different tournaments and running around the city. In my mind, we were equals. He was a lot more polished than I was, but my handle was unmatched. We weren't even rivals, like you'd think we would be. We were just homeboys who loved basketball more than anything in the world, pushing each other every day. But there's a big difference between streetball and the business of basketball. And the gap between us in terms of hype was crazy at that point in time.

Steph was *Hoop Scoop*'s No. 1 freshman in the city. His name was everywhere. Not just in one borough, like mine was, but *every* borough. Every state. They knew this dude in Staten Island. They knew him in Chicago, North Carolina, Florida. Even before the internet was popping off, he was able to build that kind of buzz at fourteen. So one day we're sitting around just kickin' it and I asked Steph, "Yo, where am I on the *Hoop Scoop* list?"

He just laughed. He's flipping the pages around.

"Uhhhhh . . ."

He's scanning his finger down the list, real exaggerated. He's squinting.

"Yo . . . lemme see."

"Stop playing, son."

"You one . . . 144."

"144?"

"144."

I didn't know anything about the politics of basketball, but I knew I was going to no Georgia Tech if I was 144th in the city. I asked Steph's father, "What do I gotta do to get in the top twenty by sophomore year?" He started explaining to me how I had to go to certain travel tournaments and get in front of certain people. I had to get up off the block and get into the right gyms in front of the right people. Then he started talking about "*Mac*Donald's, *Mac*Donald's."

"The burger joint?"

"Nah, the *All-Star Game*, son. McDonald's All-American. That's how you'll know you really made it. That's all the top high school ball players in the country."

"How many kids make it?"

"Twenty-two. Eleven on each team. Best of the best."

Now, I'm doing the math in my head. What we got in this country, *fitty states*? Plus Alaska and Hawaii, but I don't even know if they're balling out there. They shooting snowballs and coconuts? Come on, son. So let's say fitty. And you only got twenty-two dudes total on McDonald's? *Yo!* I'm 144 in the *city?! In the city?!*

I'm not even a little blip on the radar, son.

Here I am thinking I'm the shit, because I'm playing in the *park*, but in the grand scheme of things, I'm nothing.

So that was my new goal in life. McDonald's All-American. As a matter of fact, it was my only goal. I went and told my high school coach, Bill Aberer, "Yo, in four years, I want to be a McDonald's All-American. Just tell me what I gotta do?"

Bill said, "What you gotta *do*? To be All-American?"

I said, "Yeah, what I gotta do?"

"Well, first, go to church and say a prayer."

"Alright."

"Second . . . Are you serious?"

"Dead serious."

"It's not going to be easy."

"Just tell me what to do."

From that day on, I channeled all my energy into basketball. I didn't drink. I didn't smoke. I didn't go to parties. I barely slept. I spent my life in subway cars and in class and on basketball courts all over the city. My alarm went off at five thirty in the morning— one of those old plastic Casio joints that you'd have to throw across the room to snooze. I wore the same button-down Calvin Klein shirt on every single day. I had *one* shirt. I washed it on Sundays in the sink. Put my Olaf ball shorts and T-shirt in my bookbag. No breakfast. Walk ten blocks to the subway with my basketball in my hands, juking through the people on the sidewalks. Get on the train downtown. Hop a turnstile or two. No CCTV, no worries. Work out from 6:30 to 8 at my high school gym before classes started. Dribble till I was about to puke. Quick birdbath in the showers. Try to stay awake through math class. Hope one of my homeboys would let me copy the homework. Looking at the hands on that clock above the chalkboard moving impossibly slow, like, "Yo, I gotta be hallucinating. It ain't really ten thirty-six. I can't *wait* for lunch." I'd be praying they had the chicken nuggets on the menu that day. Or at least a slice of pizza. Please, don't let it be the fish sticks, son. That school lunch was my one guaranteed meal for the day, so nobody was leaving *any* leftover sides on the plate, B.

"Shamm, you wanna finish this carrot?"

"You already know, son. Give me everything. I'll eat the brussels sprouts, the green beans, the little chocolate milk, whatever. If it's free, it's for me, bro."

I'd go through a whole day of classes, change out of my ratchet shirt and tie, throw on my extra-ratchet ball shorts, and go to my varsity basketball practice. Quick birdbath again. Is the day over? Time to chill? *Hell naw* the day isn't over. I don't got a Super Nintendo waiting at home. You see what these kids are doing now on this *2K*? The NBA game? They're talking to their friends like, "Yo, meet me at the park after school." They're talking about in the damn *videogame*. They got a fake park, with fake players and fake homegirls watching in the fake bleachers. This is what these kids do now after school. Sitting at home sipping hot chocolate with the marshmallows. *Soft!* Me, I'd take the train back uptown after school and go play at the Rucker or at 145th Street Park until one o'clock in the morning. Every single day. I'm playing one-on-one against grown men and I got drug dealers betting on me. That's how you get good. That's how you learn to handle pressure. How you gonna be nervous in your little varsity game playing against St. So-and-So Academy when the night before the dealers had three thousand dollars riding on your jump shot? I never feared anything when I was in a nice gym with security guards around, because I was really out in the streets with real killers. I wasn't on no PlayStation talking shit on a headset sipping cocoa.

By the end of my freshman year, the collar on my Calvin shirt was *black* from the sweat stains. What can I say? I didn't care. It was an all-boys school. No shorties, no problem. What we talking about fashion for? I was there to *work*, son. Somehow in one of the basketball magazines I saw this advertisement for these shoes that were supposed to make you jump higher. They called them Strength Shoes. And these things looked *preposterous*. They were like normal chunky-ass Reebok shoes but with these huge weighted saucers sticking out the front. I copped the shoes and I used to wear them everywhere. Cam and Mase used to be cracking up, because they were always obsessed with looking fly all the time. Cam *invented* the color pink. He used to be wearing the pink bucket hat to the house parties before anybody was doing that. I'd show up wearing my baggy jeans with my ball shorts still on underneath, rocking these ridiculous Strength Shoes, not giving a single fuck.

Cam used to be like, "My man is walking around Harlem rocking granny's *dinner plates* on his feet. Hahahahah. Yo! You got on the *good china*, son. You *buggin'*."

I was like, "Mannn, come on. They say it helps you dunk."

"Yeah . . . I know what it *ain't* gonna help you do."

"Pssshhh. Whatever. Wait till the shorties see me dunking. Then we'll see."

They were doubled over laughing, holding their sides and shit. Six months later, I dunked a tennis ball at the park, and nobody was laughing.

Cam was looking at me like, "Damn, nigga, where can I get them Dunk Shoes?"

I didn't care about a single thing except climbing up the *Hoop Scoop* rankings. The city was my gym. Every single moment, I was on the move. I was going to or from a park or a tournament or a money game. Every borough. Nonstop.

Man, you know how much time I spent in the New York City subway just *thinking*? No phones, no Game Boys, no nothing. Just sitting on the stinky A train for two hours every day, arguing for the seven hundredth time with your boys, "Alright, alright, who would win in a freestyle . . ."

Just sitting there, *beatboxing*. That ain't just in the movies, son. We really did that shit to pass the time. Sitting on the 1 train next to grandmas and construction workers like, "One-two, one-two. Mic check. Yo, it's God MC on the mic in the place to be."

That was the only thing you had to do to pass the hours. You had a lot of time to think. A lot of time to dream. I used to actually take Mase all the way out to Coney Island with me, just so he could stand on the corner and rap for people. That was how you made a name for yourself back in the day. Nothing was in the cloud, bro. Everything was street-level. You had to really be out there holding the lighter like a microphone outside the Chinese joint, challenging anybody and everybody in Coney Island to go against the kid from Harlem. "Yo, go get your best MC. Mase will destroy 'em, B."

We used to do that everywhere. The Bronx, Queens, Staten Island. Anywhere I played ball, Mase would come and rap. The funny part was Mase always looked so young, even back then. People used to underestimate him, because he was out on the corner looking like he was somebody's *kid*, and then he would start rapping, and everybody would gather around him in awe. He used to kill so hard that he got the nickname Murder Mase.

We were on our grind. We weren't shit, but in our minds, we were already famous, you feel me?

We 144, but we *climbing*. My freshman year, I was still figuring out organized ball. There's a big difference between having a handle and being a real *point guard*. The more I played real five-on-five in a real gym with real referees and real coaches being a real pain in the ass, the more I evolved my game. They started me out on the JV squad my freshman year, and within five games, they called me up to varsity. I was the definition of a raw talent. But the real key for me was when I met Kevin Jackson. That was my sensei.

I was playing in Rucker Park one day against Juan Perez, another New York City legend. Him and Steph were the big dogs of my generation. They had all the hype. These dudes were getting the NIL money before the NIL, you feel me? Juan and his boys are changing Jordans at halftime. Swapping into a fresh pair of Jordan 4s—the low ones with the concrete on the side. They're drinking real Gatorade out of the authentic orange bucket. I was just lucky not to have holes in my shit. I'm lucky to get a sip of a Poland Spring. These dudes were *official*.

Then randomly after the game, we're sitting around bullshitting, and somebody said something about Kenny Anderson. My ears perked up. I said, "Yo, what about Kenny?"

They pointed to their coach on the sideline and said, "That's Kevin Jackson. He was Kenny's coach."

I'm like, "Word?"

They said, "Word."

I went up and introduced myself, but he was looking at me like I was a peasant, bro. He didn't know who I was. So I stalked this man for *two weeks*. I was following him around the city, begging him to let me train with him. I was like, "Yo, I'll do whatever you want. Just teach me like you taught Kenny *how to be Kenny*."

It was really like the kung fu movies where the novice keeps going to the steps of the temple to see the master and he keeps being like, "Nah, nah. You're not ready yet, grasshopper. You gotta want it more."

I was following Master Sensei all over the city. Showing up to random gyms, like, "Yo, I'll do *anything*. I don't got any money, but I'll wash the jerseys. I'll clean up the cones. I'll sweep the floors. Just teach me to be like Kenny. I'm trying to make *McDonald's*."

He was stroking his goatee, like *Hmmmmm*.

(Nah, he didn't really have a goatee, but in my mind it was like that.)

He said, "*McDonald's*, you say? It'll be hard."

"Please, sir. I need to make it outta the hood. Just help me get to college."

Finally, he broke down.

"Alright, you want to train with me? Then you come out to Queens. Every morning. Be at the gym at seven. And don't be late."

That moment—maybe more than any other moment except for Mase inspiring me to pick up a basketball for the first time— was the key to every single blessing in my life. Without Kevin Jackson, you don't know the name God Shammgod. Basketball is basketball. We'll get to that. But the thing about Kevin Jackson was that he taught me what it was to really be a man of principle. If this dude bought a sandwich at the corner store, the other half of the sandwich was in my hand before I even asked for a bite. He didn't even break his stride. He didn't even mention it. I was just holding a steak and cheese and this dude was asking me about my life. Not about ball, not about shorties, not about money. Life, son. He was like a second father and an uncle and an older brother and a coach rolled into one. He didn't even have a beard, or nothing, but it was like when this dude would be listening to you talk about your problems at home, or how your coach is an asshole, he'd be stroking that long-ass kung fu beard, you feel me? Looking into your soul, all wise, like . . . "Mmmmm."

Then once you had unloaded everything on him, about how unfair life was, and how everybody was against you, he'd drop some nugget of wisdom on you, like . . .

"Shamm?"

"Yeah?"

"Let me ask you something."

"Yeah?"

"This problem you got with your coach . . ."

"Yeah?"

"You ever try the alternative?"

"What's that?"

"The alternative."

"What's the alternative?"

"The opposite of what you doing now."

"What's that?"

"Not being a soft-ass little bitch."

"Man, fuck you."

"No, I'm serious."

"Man, come on."

"But have you tried it? You might like it. Think about it."

That was our relationship. He was always 100 percent there for me, but also 100 percent brutally honest with me. That's how every great coach should be. And I couldn't ever be mad at him, because the motherfucker always gave me the other half of his sandwich.

He saved my life. Real talk.

Once the Master Sensei started training me, it was *on*. I was a madman. I gave my life over to basketball.

I know this is going to sound almost fake. It will not even seem logistically possible. But I really went from Harlem to Queens and back to lower Manhattan every morning before school to work out with Master Sensei. Casio alarm going off like—*bllleerrrnt, bllleerrrnt, bllleerrrnt, bllleerrrnt, bllleerrrnt*—throwing that thing against the wall, like: It can't be morning again. It's not possible.

Put the Calvin Klein shirt back on. Yo, my *fingers* are sore. Everything hurts. Hop the turnstile. Back on the train again. Conductor coming on the speakers: "Due to a malfunction at . . ."

Yo!!!!! THIS CAN'T BE MY LIFE. I SHOULDA BEEN MOVING PACKS. I TAKE IT ALL BACK.

But once I got that basketball in my hands, all was right with the world. I was at peace. Once I started working with Kevin Jackson, my game just took off. He tapped into something in me, and it was more than the physical side. It was the mental side too. Kev showed me how to see the whole picture on the basketball court—the entire chessboard. The most important thing about being a point guard is that it ain't about *you*. I know that sounds crazy coming from the guy who is famous all around the world for putting a basketball between his legs, but the reality is, doing crossovers is 1 percent of being a point guard. The other 99 percent is being selfless. Even when you are doing a crossover, the point of it is not to make the crowd go apeshit. It's not to get a shoe deal. It's not to big yourself up. Nah, go and look at all my highlights. Ninety-nine percent of the time after I did one of my moves, and I shook the defender, you know what I did? I passed the ball to the open man for the easy bucket. When you're just a streetball player, you always try to be the hero. You draw all the attention to you, and then you try to finish at the rim yourself. But when you're a real point guard, you're moving around the opponent's chess pieces on the board so that you can free up your teammates. That's what Kev taught me. He taught me how to be a real point god, not just a sideshow. But don't take my word for it. I got receipts for everything. We can run it through a hood fact-check. Literally, you can ask Tyronn Lue. We played AAU against each other back in the day. (I know, I'm the Harlem Forrest Gump. I been around everybody.)

We were in the NBA Bubble during Covid a couple years ago, and Ty was coaching for the Clippers. I was coaching for the Mavericks. (More on that later. My life is crazy. Just go with the flash-forward, y'all. Don't ask questions.)

So there were a couple of players and coaches standing around before the warm-ups—a few from the Clippers, a few from the Mavs. Just catching up, telling stories. And Ty was cracking them up, man. He's pointing over at me like, "Man, y'all kids want to talk to me about *Iverson*? You see this guy here? When we played Shamm in high school, we thought he was an *alien*. He did a crossover and he shook our whole zone. He went one way, five dudes went the other way."

You thought I was exaggerating with the kung fu master story, huh? Nah, I was doing some *Crouching Tiger, Hidden Dragon* shit with the basketball back then. I had dudes flying up into the rafters when I crossed 'em up. They was doin' triple backflips. Ask Ty! Ask anybody!

By the end of my sophomore year, I was a *bad* man. The new *Hoop Scoop* came out, and I was top twenty in the city. Steph, of course, was still numero uno. I owe Steph so much, because we played the same position, and he could've been the ultimate hater. But instead, he was my ultimate pusher. He was the one who was always telling me, "You can make McDonald's, Shamm. I'm *telling* you, you just gotta keep working."

What's funny is that I was way more famous in the streets than I was in the gyms. I had been a household name at the Rucker long before any D1 coaches started calling up my moms. Long before I was getting any recruiting letters, I had little kids imitating the crossovers I was doing at the parks, screaming out, "Yo, there go Shammgod!" I was signing autographs in the hood before I even had a scholarship offer. I was a hood celebrity, and there's a lot that comes with that. Girls start liking you a little too easily, you feel me? You're wearing Tims and a hoodie and they're telling you they like your style. Come on, queen. You've known me since I was begging for the last chicken wing. The energy starts changing. People start trying to give you money, with no strings attached. But there's *always* strings. Being a hood celebrity is no different than being a real celebrity, except you take a comma off everything. You're a thousandaire now. You're getting free Nikes instead of free Gucci. You're the provider for your family at that point, and you gotta put the food on the table, even if it's just beef 'n' broccoli. I tell people all the time: it's hard having money. And it's hard having no money. The best place you can be is when you got enough cheddar that you don't have to look at the price on the cereal box. When you got *enough*. Enough for you and your people, but not for the whole hood. That's the sweet spot. You know what's an *amazing* feeling? You know what's even better than sitting in the front seat of a new BMW? You know what's even better than buying a Rolex and having the mother-fucker at the register call you "Mister"? *Way* before you get that rich. *Way* before that. When you get to look your little sister in her eyes and you say, "Yo, what you wanna eat tonight? It's on me. The Chinese spot? Get whatever you want. Let's fuck up the whole the menu. It's your world."

You're not even out of the hood yet, but you're in heaven.

Back then, when I went to sleep at night, I didn't dream about going to the NBA. I couldn't even really envision what that meant. All I ever dreamed about was to make enough money that my mother didn't have to worry about anything. Step one was going to college for free.

I remember my mom saying to me one day, "Wait, they're gonna *pay* for this? For you to go to school? For *basketball*."

"Ya, Ma."

"For *basketball*. That's *amazing*. Remember when you came home from school, talking about, 'Mom, mom, mom—there's this sport called basketball'?"

"Ya, Ma, that was only four years ago. I used to just pick up the ball and *run* in PE class. Now we gonna get you a nice house. We gonna get up out of here."

"But I like it here."

"Ya, Ma . . . Me too."

What's crazy is that around that same time, between our sophomore and junior year, Mase, Big L, and Cam'ron were all starting to blow up in New York too. They started this group called Children of the Corn with our boys Herb McGruff and Bloodshed from the block. They got into a real studio a couple times to record some tracks, which was a big deal. They used to sit outside Willie Burger and sell their mixtape for five bucks to the hustlers. Day by day, they started getting more buzz around the city. Our junior year, Puff Daddy started coming around to talk to Mase. Sometimes he would bring around this huge motherfucker from Brooklyn with a funny way of talking. He had just signed the dude to Bay Boy Records. They were working on a little album called *Ready to Die*. When I met the dude, he sounded just like me when I first moved to Harlem. "Yo, I'm from *Brooklyn*, son. Name's Biggie."

It was the legend. The GOAT. The Notorious BIG.

The funny thing was, I was a huge *2Pac* fan at that time.

I remember arguing with Mase and Jay-Z and Big L at the park, like, "Nah, Pac is *way* better than Biggie. Come on, son."

What can I say? I was always a contrarian! But you gotta understand, when all of this is happening, in terms of the *hood*, I was
on the same wavelength as these dudes. I was never starstruck.
Biggie hadn't totally blown up yet. He was just a dude I knew. Jay
was just a dude I knew. Puff was a record producer, like a million
other record producers. Honestly, Biggie was trying to meet *me*.
I don't say that to be arrogant. I'm just stating facts. He loved
basketball and he used to come around to our high school games
just to kick it. There's this famous picture of me, Steph, and Biggie in the tunnel after a game, and Biggie got the dark sunglasses
on and the XXL track suit and the pinkie rings. Biggie is *doing the
most*. He's flashing the M hand sign for Junior Mafia. Steph is just
looking stone-cold like Steph always looks. His expression is like,
"Yo, I know I'm the man. I'm number one in the *nation*." And me,
I'm just staring off into the distance, looking like I'm thinking
about *dinner* or something. Like it's just another day.

It's crazy to look back on that picture now, because if I knew
then what I know now, I'd have probably been doing the most.
I'd have been grinning ear to ear, taking a picture with one of the
greatest to ever do it. But what I love about that picture is that it's
so authentic. It's a moment frozen in time. Back then, in 1993, I
was just Shamm, and Steph was just Steph, and Big was just Big.
Three kids from New York City with some dreams. The story
was still waiting to be written. Honestly, it all happened so fast for
me that I didn't know how to be anybody *but* myself.

By the end of my junior year, I was No. 2 in the city behind
Steph.

Mase was about to sign with Bad Boy.

Big was about to drop *Ready to Die*.

It was 1994. A new era. We ran the city. We were the culture.

Then I heard the three words that changed my life. My girl called me up out of the blue. We'd only been seeing each other on and off for a few months. It wasn't serious. We were just kids. We were more like friends. For some reason, she was crying. I thought maybe somebody had died or something.

Then she said, "Shamm, I'm pregnant."

I hadn't even turned seventeen yet. And I was about to become a father.

Everything in life happens for a reason. I know it sounds like a cliche, but you can trust me on that. See, only motherfuckers who have lived a *real* life can verify a philosophical statement like that. And I'm a real motherfucker, and I'm telling you.

When I say everything happens for a reason, it doesn't always mean it happens the way you want it to happen. But it happens the way it's supposed to happen, whether we understand God's plan or not. Case in point: summer 1994. That summer was one of the most pivotal moments of my life. I'm going into my senior year. Still don't know where I'm going to college. I got a son on the way. I've got siblings depending on me. I've got my mother depending on me. Everything in my life was hanging in the balance.

I didn't want to be one of those "used to be's." See, I grew up in a neighborhood with a lot of Used to Be stories.

"Yo, that dude used to be number one in the city, but then he got locked up."

"This dude used to be going D-One, but then he had a kid."

"Man, I'm telling you. He don't look like it now, but homeboy over there on the corner selling crack rock used to be the best point guard in the city back in the day."

"But then what happened?"

"Then he got shot."

But then. But then. But then . . .

There were so many guys who got so close to making it out— who could see that light at the end of the tunnel—and then they got pulled back into the street life, or they got lazy, or they started sniffing that powder, you feel me? "Just a little bit, it ain't gonna hurt nobody. It's just one party. What's the worst that can happen?" In the hood? *A lot.* I wasn't going to let that happen to me. I wasn't gonna be a Used to Be story. I had too much riding on it. I had no safety net. It was just me against the world.

Going into my senior year, my father was actually just getting out of prison, but we kept our distance. I had a lot of anger in my heart toward him. To be clear, my father was no cliche. He had a good heart. He got his degree in prison, and when he came out, he worked for twenty years on the straight and narrow as a tech for Verizon. But when he was coming out of jail, I couldn't let go of the past. I felt like a lot of my mother's problems with substance abuse started as soon as he got locked up. I blamed him for putting me in a situation where I had to fight for my mother's safety with another man in our home. Maybe it wasn't fair to him, but I couldn't get over that. *You really left an eight-year-old kid at home to be the protector? Really? I don't care what you were dealing with in your life. I don't care if it was complicated. You let that* happen? *And we're supposed to be cool now?* Nah. I'm sorry. I wasn't ready. It took me a long time to let go of that hurt. At seventeen, I damn sure wasn't ready.

What I didn't know until years later was that he had tried to rekindle things with my mom when he got out of prison. But unfortunately, she was still with my stepfather, and he took exception to it. The whole thing was straight out of *General Hospital*, son. One thing led to another, and they got into a fistfight one night over my mother. From that day on, my father kept a respectful distance. He would still come around, but everything just felt off with me and him.

You know what it was like?

It was exactly like that movie *He Got Game*.

Remember Denzel with the little mini afro, just tearing shit up on the screen, trying to connect with his son?

Sounds a little bit familiar, right?

You know why it was like that movie? Because it *was* that movie, son.

See, this is where I tell you another fact about my life that seems fake. But I don't do fake. I told you—I'm the hood Forrest Gump. Nothing happens in basketball without me being on the scene, son. Go and ask Spike Lee, and he'll tell you. See, Spike was coming up to Harlem all the time during '94 and '95 to watch me and Steph and Felipe Lopez. He was just coming off *Malcolm X*, and he wanted his next project to be on basketball and the city, because he could see what we were doing. He could see the power in it. It was bigger than basketball. It was bigger than scholarships and money and girls. We were the *culture*. He came around all the time and he heard me and Steph's stories. If you don't believe me, do me a favor . . .

I can't remember the name of the main character. What *was* his name? Damn . . . My memory ain't what it used to be!

It was Jesus, right?

That's it. Jesus Shuttlesworth.

Sound familiar?

Spike took elements of both of me and Steph's backgrounds for *He Got Game*. Spike originally wanted both me and Steph to be in the movie, but by the time they started filming, we were already in college, and we couldn't make it work, so Ray Allen ended up being cast as Jesus. People ask me all the time what I think about *He Got Game*, and it's like they want me to be bitter that Ray played the part and got so much love for it, or that they took our real struggle and made it into fiction. But honestly, all I feel is gratitude. A lot of what you see in the movie is exaggerated. I definitely never had two fly shorties waiting for me in the bed on my recruiting visits, I'm sorry to say. But there's elements of the movie that are so raw and authentic. The thing for me that hit home the most is seeing Denzel Washington playing my father, coming straight out of jail, trying to have a relationship with me. I know it's supposed to be Jesus, but that's me. That's *him*. That iconic scene where they're playing one-on-one at the park—that was just like me and my father at that time. Just the tension and the resentment, but still having that love underneath . . .

When you watch that scene, you can feel the hurt that Jesus felt.

That was *my* hurt.

I respected my father. But I never wanted to be him.

As soon as I found out I was going to be a father, I made a promise to myself: Whatever I do in this life, whether I'm broke or I'm a millionaire, whether I make it to the NBA or I'm working at the airport, I'm going to make sure my son never has to worry about anything. My son comes before *everything*. He's never going to see me behind glass, asking the guards if he can give me a hug. You would've thought I would've been scared out of my mind, but I felt like I was on top of the world when he was on the way. My son gave me a focus, and a deeper purpose before he even came into the world.

He was due at the end of November, right in the middle of my senior year. I had a few months to solidify my whole future. I moved in with my girlfriend's parents, because they had a real stable, beautiful thing going in their home. They lived in the Bronx in a nice house. Her mother was a middle school principal and her father was a corrections officer, so there was no messing around. *Zero.* "When the sun goes down, all we doin' in this house is *homework*, son. Sharpen up your pencils."

First thing her mom said to me when I moved in: "How's your grades?"

"Uhhhh . . . Like a C. Maybe C-plus. Yeah, definitely *C-plus*, you know what I'm saying?"

"Mmm*hmmm*. Yeah, we're done with the Cs. We're skipping over the Bs too. We're getting *As* in this house, son."

She was exactly like Aunt Viv from *The Fresh Prince*. She had that same aura. Super precise, super put-together. I moved in and upended everything they had going on, but she didn't even blink. She just treated me like her own son. She *loved* me. That's the best you can give anybody. To this day, I call her "moms." It was like God knew exactly what I needed in my life at that point. I had never seen an example of stability like that growing up. Once I had that feeling of security? Once I knew that I was living for something more than just myself? I'm getting home-cooked meals? My basketball shorts are smelling like fresh laundry? Remember that old commercial with the white teddy bear? For the fabric softener? Man, Aunt Viv had the *Snuggle Bear* popping out the laundry basket. Now my socks are coming out warm and toasty. Who gonna stop me now that I got fresh socks on my feet?

That season, I exploded. I went Super-*Saiyan*, son. I was going *crazy*. I was hitting dudes with crossovers that were so filthy that all that was left was a pair of smoking Js on the pavement. Police had to come and sketch the chalk outlines for motherfuckers in Rucker Park. I was leaving bodies out there. I was *murdering*. And that was just in the *streets*, mind you. If you were a little soft high school *varsity* motherfucker? An *honor roll* motherfucker? If you weren't really about that life, and you were lining up across from me slapping the floor, talking shit, trying to press me in front of the cheerleaders?

Yo. Call the coroner. Call the undertaker. Please pray for this kid's family.

I wasn't even a father yet, but I had a hundred *sons*. Every camp I went to, every tournament, I was making the suburban kids cry. I was making these prep school stars question their choices in life. "Go play lacrosse, son. Go join the marching band. You not built for this." Once I was eating those home-cooked sweet potatoes from Aunt Viv, there was nothing you could do to stop me.

From five o'clock in the morning until eleven o'clock at night, it was me versus the world. At 6 a.m., I was working out with Master Sensei Kevin Jackson. Then I'd go to school and be destroying these tests—I'm talking straight As, across the board—and by 3 p.m. I'd be either at practice or at the parks. On nights when I didn't have a game, I'd go to the gym at the Kips Ball Mall with Aunt Viv and we'd get on a StairMaster workout. She hooked me up with the guest pass and we were on our *Suzanne Somers*, son. That was my nighttime grind. I was going to do anything and everything to get my ass a scholarship.

By that summer of 1994, I was starting to get some shine on a national level. I remember I got my first college letter from James Madison University. I didn't even know where James Madison was, but I knew it was D1. I told my moms, "Hey, you don't gotta worry anymore. No matter what happens, we already got one in the bag. I'm gonna get my degree for free. We'll be doing good soon."

My son's mother was rock solid about everything. She and Aunt Viv were always telling me, "We know what you gotta do. You go to college, and we'll hold it down here. Don't worry about nothing." It was a unique era in that sense. That crack era was so bad that it's like everybody who survived it was just trying to fig-ure out how to go to school or build a business and make a better life. It's so funny to me now, because I see my own son having *his own son now*, all these years later, and this motherfucker is over thirty years old, and I'm looking at him like, *Yo, how can you be a father? Do you even know how to do your own laundry? What are you feeding this kid? Is it organic? You gotta be checking those labels. They be lying.*

I'm *stressed*, just looking at him holding my grandson, you feel me?

The circle of life, man. Just like my father. Just like his father before him, probably.

But for me, back then, as a sixteen-year-old father, I literally felt no fear. If ignorance is bliss, I was the dumbest dude in Harlem. I was having the time of my *life* with my little homie.

Around that time, my name was starting to percolate in the big national basketball magazines. I was moving up in the world, but I was still in the shadow of Steph and Felipe Lopez in the city, and then outside the city you had generational talent like Kevin Garnett and Paul Pierce and Chauncey Billups. I was still being looked at as a "street player" in a lot of ways. Basketball for me was still pure. I wasn't looking at it as a business. Steph and his brothers, they were always looking at it so clinically. They had it all figured out. I remember they were always talking about "ABCD. *ABCD.* You gotta go to ABCD Camp to get on people's radar, Shamm."

I'm like, "ABCD? What we doing, *Hooked on Phonics*? We going to summer school? The hell you talking about?"

"Nah, nah. ABCD Camp with Sonny Vaccaro. He's like the Godfather of high school basketball. He's Don Corleone. It's the biggest camp in America, son. All the best players go to ABCD. All the college coaches are there. You even get free Nikes, B."

So that summer, I finally got the big invite to this mythical ABCD Camp. It was up in New Jersey at this college in the suburbs, and we were staying in some dorm rooms for the week. I get there and check in, and I find out I'm sharing a room with this kid from *France* or somewhere. He's rocking the baldie like 2Pac. Lanky dude. He'd be smiling one second, scowling the next. He had what you might call an aura.

I said, "Alright, what's good, France? You wanna go get some Chinese food?"

He was always like, "Man, stop calling me France. I'm from *Italy*."

But when you're young and stupid, and you've never been outside of the country, everything in Europe is just France to you. So everybody at the camp was always like, "Alright, France, whatever you say."

This dude had an interesting personality. At the dorm, he was superchill. Real quiet. All he wanted to do was talk about basketball. But once he came through the double doors of that gym, it was like he transformed into a different person.

Now this dude walked like Jordan.

Now this dude talked like Jordan.

This dude *chewed gum* like Jordan. Right out the side of his mouth like MJ—aggressive, *chompin'* on that shit—argh argh argh argh.

Then he gets on the court with some of the best high school players in the country, and what's he doing? This kid is shooting *all* the basketballs, man. *Allllll of* the basketballs. He's getting doubled, he's getting tripled, and he's shooting that signature MJ turnaround fadeaway.

He's even got the *tongue* hanging out like Mike.

Of course, everybody's clowning him.

"Alright, France. Chill, brother. *Chill.* You think you're MJ? *You not gonna be no MJ!*"

He's on the sideline with the white towel over his head, sitting on the bleachers, not saying a word to anybody, just *super intense*. He's even staring off into the middle distance just like MJ, chompin' on that gum with a vengeance—argh argh argh argh.

I'm looking at the other guys like, "Yo, where did they find this kid?? He can ball a little bit, but he's actually crazy."

So after the first day of the camp, this kid's father comes up to me, talking about, "Hey, I would really appreciate it if you could show my son some of your moves. He can't dribble like you. He can do everything else, but he really needs to work on his handle."

Turns out France's pops is actually a coach at La Salle University. In my head, I'm still kind of in my feelings, because this kid is shooting *all* the shots, but I'm not one to burn a bridge with any D1 coach, so I told his father, "Alright, cool. I'll show him some stuff tomorrow morning before the camp starts. But listen, I come to the gym early. Like, *early* early. We start at six a.m. If he doesn't wake up, then that's on him."

His pops is cracking up.

"Oh, don't worry, he'll be up."

Remember, we're *rooming* together. We go to sleep that night, and I'm like: "Yo, France. Remember. Six o'clock. I'm setting the alarm for five thirty, son."

"Cool."

"Cool."

"Good night."

"Good night, France. Sleep tight."

This prep school motherfucker ain't waking up.

The Casio goes off at 5:25. *Blllerrrrnnntttt. Blllleeerrrrttttt. Blllllerrrrrnt.*

I bop the top. Shhhhh. It's pitch black. I'm quiet as a church mouse. I look across the room. No France. Just a mountain of bedsheets.

What the fuck?

He in the shower or something?

"France! Yo, France?!"

His shoes are gone. His bag is gone. His basketball is gone.

Oh hell naw.

I walk to the gym. Sun still coming up. Sleep crusting in my eyes. I'm thinking there's *no way* France is gonna be in there. He went back home. He quit. He couldn't hang with the big dogs. *Soft.* See, *this what happens when you try to play with New Y—*

I push open the double doors, and this dude is out on the court all alone, in the dark. Back in the day when you'd break into a gym and turn on the lights at the circuit breaker, they took like thirty minutes to warm up. They'd be buzzing and shit.

It was like that. Dude is in the dark, running full-court sprints, already in a full sweat. He's even *dripping* like Jordan. He got the impossibly big MJ sweat drops on his forehead, like you see in a cartoon. Them big old water drops. He turns to me, and he's grinning.

He says, "You're late."

I'm like, "Morning, France. You tired yet?"

"Man, stop calling me France. You know my name."

"Yo, what is it again?"

"My name's *Kobe*."

Hahahahaha. *Yes, sir.*

Who else did you think was at the gym at five thirty in the morning, shooting all the shots? My roommate was none other than Mr. Kobe Bean Bryant. My *man*.

I mean, just to put it in perspective: At the time, Kobe was already blowing up a tiny bit around Philly, but he was a year younger than me, and in my mind I'm like, *I been blowed up. I'm the man around here. I'm gonna run this kid ragged.*

He's like, "You need to stretch?"

I'm like, "Son, I'm just doing a favor for your pops."

"Cool."

"Cool."

"You ready to dribble?"

"I've been ready."

So we're at this gym at six o'clock in the morning doing these insane dribbling drills, and we *both* think we're the shit. We're *both* some crazy, obsessive competitors. *Nobody* is trying to blink, man. And we're not playing one-on-one or H-O-R-S-E or nothing like that. There were zero shots going up. *Nah, we're in my world now, Kobe.* We're just dribbling for two hours straight.

We're nose-to-nose, staring each other down, like: *doot-doot-doot-doot*, left hand, right hand, crossover, left hand, right hand, *doot-doot-doot-doot.*

We're tryna see who's gonna drop first.

We're tryna *dribble* each other to death.

It went on like that for literally like ninety-five minutes straight. No water breaks. No stopping.

I'm thinking, *Yo, this European motherfucker is* relentless.

The camp counselors finally came in to start setting up the cones and shit, and they were looking at us like, *Yo! What the* hell? *Gym don't open till eight! How'd you get in here?*

Doot-doot-doot-doot. Doot-doot-doot-doot. Doot-doot-doot-doot.

Doot-doot-doot-doot.

Doot-doot-doot-doot.

Doot-doot-doot-doot.

"You tired, France?"

"Fuck you."

"Eyes up."

"Fuck you."

"Bend them knees, France."

"Fuck you."

We left two identical sweat puddles on the floor that you could've gone swimming in. He never quit. He's on the bleachers, drinking his Gatorade like MJ.

"You tired *now*, France?"

"Nope."

"We doin' this again tomorrow?"

"Yep. I'll be here at five thirty."

"Five . . . *Yo*. You crazy, you know that? You for *real* crazy."

"Yep."

That was the start of a great, great, great, great friendship between me and Kobe. A bond that's *forever*. We had no *idea* what we were gonna become, what we were gonna do in life, you know what I'm saying? Well, Kobe knew. He was gonna be MJ, *for real*. The only other person I'd ever seen who was so obsessed with greatness like that was Steph.

I went back to Harlem after that camp, and I was telling Mase and Cam and all my boys, "Yo, you wouldn't believe this kid I met at ABCD. He literally thinks he's Jordan. He taught himself to *sweat* like MJ."

They said, "Word?"

I said, "I'm telling you. You'd love this kid. He's crazy as hell."

"What's his name?"

"Kobe or some shit."

"Kobe? What kind of name is that?"

"I dunno, B. We were all calling him France."

"What you talking about, he *sweat* like Jordan?"

"B, I'm telling you. He got the Jordan droplets."

Next time I saw Kobe, I was playing at this camp up in Providence, Rhode Island, a couple months later. It was all the big dogs—Vince Carter, Tim Thomas, Robert "Tractor" Traylor. Kobe was still kind of an enigma, because he was a year younger than most of us. I remember my coach asking me before the game, "Yo, what's the deal with the Kobe kid? Is he really that nice?"

I said, "Yeah, he's pretty nice. He thinks he's Jordan, but he plays exactly like Grant Hill."

He just laughed, like, "Grant Hill?"

"Grant Hill. For real."

"I don't care who he plays like, he ain't doing *nothing* against us today."

Of course, Kobe went off. He was killing us.

At halftime, my coach is looking at me wild-eyed like, "Man, WHO IS THIS KID?"

I said, "I told you! Crazy motherfucker from *France*."

I kind of lost track of Kobe after that, because I had so much going on my senior year and then eventually going off to college that I barely watched TV, and I definitely wasn't on the internet. Back then things were a lot more mysterious. I remember coming back to Harlem after my freshman year, and I'm sitting around on the block just chilling, and everyone is coming up to me like, "Yo! Your man Kobe is putting in *work*."

I said, "What you mean?"

They're like, "He's going straight to the league. From high school, B. He's number one in the nation."

"What? Nah, Tim Thomas is number one."

"I'm telling you, B. You haven't been watching ESPN?"

"I don't watch TV, son."

"He's going to the league."

"Man, what? All he wanna do is *shoot*."

I was being a hater. *France ain't going to the league at seventeen. Come on, son. That's ridiculous.*

The next day, I go to the barbershop, and they turn on the TV, and I see my boy France. Grinning ear to ear. Wearing a tuxedo. Paparazzi cameras going off.

What the hell?

Everybody in the barber shop is cracking up.

"Yo!!! Shamm, it's your boy!!!"

This motherfucker is at the prom with *Brandy*. He literally brought Moesha as his prom date. In 1995? That was the ultimate flex.

All I could do was laugh. *Brandy, son? How you even get homegirl's number?*

The whole barbershop on my ass: "Aaaaahhhhhhhhh!!! Yoooooo!! Your *boy!!*"

That summer, everywhere I went in Harlem, any time that song "I Wanna Be Down" came on the radio, everybody just started cracking up and pointing at me.

"Ahhhhhhhh!!! Yooooo!!! Shamm, it's ya boy!!! You don't think he got game, huh?!"

I couldn't even be mad. I'm like: *Yo, alright. You win, France. Respect. You still can't dribble, but you win this round, B.*

Dude was special. He was one of one. To this day, I can't think of Kobe without getting a little bit choked up, because we were kindred spirits. There was a connection there that was so deep, and that would go on for years. Back then, when we were just kids, I had no idea the kind of impression I had made on him.

Years later, after he passed away, I ran into his sister, and we were just reminiscing. She said, "You know, Kobe came home from that one camp, and we just kept hearing this *name* all the time. Shammgod, Shammgod, Shammgod. We'd be at the dinner table, and all Kobe talked about was basketball. We'd be eating and he'd say, 'You gotta see what Shammgod can do with the ball.' Shammgod, Shammgod, Shammgod."

I said, "Word? I had no idea."

She said, "Your name was mythical in our house. He used to grab a rolled-up sock and put it between his legs in the living room, like 'This is what Shammgod do.'"

The fact that my name used to ring out in the streets—that gives me a lot of pride.

But the fact that my name used to ring out around the dinner table of an NBA legend . . . that's a deeper feeling. That gives me so much gratitude. All I can do is thank God for putting Kobe in my life.

For some people, basketball is their stress. It's what keeps them up at night. It's what makes them nervous. For me and Kobe, it was a relief. It was the sanctuary.

When we had the ball in our hands, all was right in the world.

Kindred spirits. How many of them does God put in your life? You gotta appreciate the time you have with them, because it's always shorter than you think.

My mother had never seen me play a basketball game. She had too much to deal with in her own life. All through high school, she was still battling her demons. But we had a deal. I was always telling her, "If I make McDonald's All-American, you're going to come see me, right?"

"What's this thing you're always talking about? You're playing outside a McDonald's?"

"No, Ma, it's a big deal. It's all the best high school players in the country. You play in a big arena."

"Madison Square Garden?"

"Yeah, something like that, Ma."

"My *baby's* gonna be doing that? In front of all those people?"

"Maybe, Ma. We'll see. I'm doing my best."

"Wow. That's amazing. Do I have to get on a plane?"

"Yeah. You gotta promise me, Ma. If I make it, you're coming, right?"

"I promise. I promise."

I know this sounds crazy now, in the days of social media and cell phones and everything, but my mom really didn't understand why people would want to fly a seventeen-year-old around the country to play a basketball game. Madison Square Garden, that was like a whole different world for us in Harlem. My mom had never even been on an airplane before. In her mind, basketball was just something I did down at the park to stay out of trouble. Even when I started getting college recruiting letters, she couldn't believe that all these schools would want to pay for my tuition just because I could put a ball in a hoop. When I was talking about "McDonald's, McDonald's, McDonald's," she would just laugh.

"They gonna give you a free cheeseburger too? Get me a Big Mac."

But she promised me that if I was an All-American, she would come see me play.

By the beginning of my senior season, I was the No. 2 point guard in the city behind Steph. There was just one problem: McDonald's was nationwide. There's two teams—an East and a West team. That's eleven players from the whole eastern half of the *country*. So everybody was real with me. They were telling me, "Yo, there's no way that they're going to take two point guards from the same city. They're only gonna take the number one in New York, and you know who that's gonna be."

For some reason, I never got down about it. I don't know why, but I had this inner belief that if I played good enough my senior year, I'd force them to take both me and Steph. We're talking about *New York City*, B. They're gonna take somebody from Jersey or from Philly or God forbid from North Carolina over me?

They still shootin' on the peach basket down there. Nah. I'm gonna make them break the rules for us, because we're just that nice. We're gonna be undeniable.

So I went to work. I was training every waking hour. Then right as my senior basketball season was starting, on November 27, 1994, God gave me the greatest gift of my life. My son was born. God Shammgod Jr. At three weeks old, he was already at my high school game, wrapped up in a little blanket, cheering for daddy. Aunt Viv took him to every single game the rest of that season, and he became like our team's little mascot. Everybody knew him. You know what's crazy? He'd never even cry. He'd just be looking up with his eyes all big, taking it all in. He was literally raised in the gym. The first thing I did after every game, whether I dropped 10 or 30, was to run up into the bleachers and give him a hug.

"What you think, little man? Did daddy kill 'em tonight?"

"Gahhhh. *Gahhhhhh*."

He's looking up at me like I'm his hero.

What a feeling.

To this day, I always tell him, "You know what you did for me? You saved my life."

He also saved my relationship with my own father. Once my son was born, and he became a grandfather, everything changed. He was rock solid. He was on the spot for everything. *Diapers? Yo, I'm already out the door. I'm going to the corner store. I got it. Babysitter? I'm there. Tell me what to feed little dude.* He was *on* it. The way that he would look at his grandson . . . It was crazy. My son would laugh, and my father would laugh. My son would cry, and my father would be damn near crying. It's like my father *softened*, just holding his grandson in his arms. This super strong, super radical Black Panther—my son used to make this dude melt, man. I started seeing my father in such a different light when I became a father, and I finally started giving him a little bit of grace.

That season on the court, I was unstoppable. Love will always take you to another level. Your shoes be feeling a little lighter when you're playing for somebody else. There's this picture of us that I love. I had just won Most Outstanding Player at this tournament in DC, and I'm smiling for the camera with the trophy in one arm and my son in the other.

I was seventeen.

My son is in his thirties now, and I can't imagine *him* having a son right now. I don't know how I was doing it at seventeen, but I was doing it, and I loved every second of it.

My entire goal that season, other than making McDonald's, was for Kenny Anderson to come see one of my games. I was still working out with Master Sensei Kevin Jackson all the time, and I was always showing him my stats in the newspaper and telling him, "Does Kenny know what I'm doing? Can you pass a message to him? Just tell him to come down to the city and see one of my games."

Kenny was already in the NBA at that point, playing for the Nets right up in New Jersey. Master Sensei came back to me a week later.

"I talked to Kenny. He said he doesn't know no Shammgod. He

knows *Stephon Marbury*. But he never heard of no Shammgod."

He was gassing me up.

I said, "For real? Well, send a message back to Kenny. Tell him I'm about to drop fifty for him. *Fitty*, okay? *Fitty*."

I went out a few weeks later and I dropped 50 on some unsuspecting high school motherfuckers.

I brought the newspaper into the gym and gave it to Master Sensei.

I said, "Send this to Kenny."

A couple weeks later, I'm in the gym warming up before some random high school game, and all of a sudden I hear a commotion in the bleachers. People be pulling out pens and paper. They're screaming. It's Kenny Anderson. He came to the game without telling me. Man, I was so locked in. I mean, I used to look in the mirror and pretend to *be* this dude. Now he's watching me? Oh, you already *know*. I'm putting on a show.

I dropped 55 that night. *Fitty-five. Five five.* In a thirty-two-minute high school game. I was levitating, bro.

Kenny came up to me after the game to shake my hand, and his eyes were buggin' out of his head. He said, "Yoooooooooooo! I never *seen* a high school game like that in my life!"

I said, "You know the name Shammgod now?"

He said, "Man, you're gonna do great things. Just keep working, son."

That's the moment I really *knew*. I was going to college. I was going to play pro ball. I was going to make a living out of this game. I was going to change my family's situation. Everything I ever dreamed about when I was lying on that bench in the alleyway in the middle of the projects, all alone . . . It wasn't a dream no more. It was right in front of me.

At the end of that season, I was sitting in my third-period science class, just trying to stay awake. Teacher is up there talking about neutrons, and I'm just trying to make it to the chicken nuggets at lunch, bro. I've been up since 5 a.m. At that point I'm doing *three-a-days* at the gym. I'm getting straight As. I'm an honor roll student thanks to Aunt Viv, and so I'm sleeping like four hours a night, tops. By third period every day, I'm hitting the wall, you feel me?

So I'm dozing off, when all of a sudden the principal comes over the loudspeaker.

"Attention, students. Attention, staff . . ."

Oh, snap. What's going on? We got a fire drill?

"We have an announcement to make. We just got some news about one of our very own students. The 1995 McDonald's All-American team has just been announced, and I'm happy to announce that it includes our very own *Mister* . . ."

As soon as I heard ". . . Shammgod" I blacked out. I just started crying.

All the students started pounding on the desks. Not just in our class, but you could hear it booming down the hall from the other classrooms. All the teachers came into the room and started clapping. It was like the ending of one of those corny high school movies, only it was for real. People were chanting my name. And I was just sobbing, man.

You can't help but think about the whole journey, when you

get a moment like that. My whole life flashed before my eyes. I thought, *I can't wait to tell Steph. I can't wait to tell Mase. I can't wait to get home and tell my mother. She's actually gonna see me play.*

That was probably the proudest moment of my life. When I told her that I made it, I remember she said, "Wow, that's amazing. I better go get a nice dress, huh? If my baby's gonna be on national TV, I need to be looking nice."

She had her demons, but in my eyes, my mom could never do anything wrong, because I knew that she had a pure soul. Everybody needs a number one fan in life. I was my mother's. I remember she was so nervous about leaving New York.

She said, "How much does it cost for a plane ticket?"

I said, "No, Ma, you don't understand. They're flying *us* out. They got a fancy banquet and everything. We're gonna be eating good. Wait till you see how big they do it at these basketball banquets. Steak and shrimp, Ma. It's *crazy.*"

She just started crying. I think she couldn't believe that her baby was really opening up this whole new world. She still remembered when I was jumping off the arm of the couch back in Crown Heights, doing the Superfly Snuka elbow drop onto my little brother. She remembered when we had nothing. It was just yesterday.

I'll never forget landing in St. Louis for the McDonald's Game and meeting up with all the guys. That '95 roster looks *fake.* It's looking like something out of a videogame. It seems impossible that all these legends could've been together in the same place at the same time. But that's just my life. I attract greatness.

Kevin Garnett. Vince Carter. Stephon Marbury. Paul Pierce.

Chauncey Billups. Shareef Abdur-Rahim. Robert "Tractor" Traylor. Antawn Jamison. Ron Mercer.

I mean, do kids nowadays even understand how *nice* Shareef Abdur-Rahim was behind the arc? He was the first power forward who could dribble and shoot treys and do it all. He was the prototype of all the dudes you love watching now. We used to call him "the president" because we'd all be wiling out like dumb teenagers and Shareef would be sitting back in the corner reading a book, pondering the meaning of life.

The '95 McDonald's Game was a movie. You had generational talent all together in the same gym at the same time, and the craziest part was that we were all *boys*. Everybody got along great. You would think that with so much ego in the same room at that age, it would be a recipe for disaster, but everybody was kicking it. Those are the best times in life—when you are just on the precipice of making it. When you already *know* who you are, but you're not that person yet. When your whole future is stretched out in front of you, and you're just talking with your boys, dreaming about how everything is gonna be, talking shit:

"Oh, Tractor Traylor got the *bag*, huh? Hey, don't let the NCAA see what you driving, big dog!"

"KG going straight to the league! KG, can I borrow some money, big homie? I gotta pay my cable bill!"

"Luther Clay over here going to Purdue. Ain't that an all-boys school, son? What the homegirls like in *Indiana*?"

"Shammgod, where you going? *Providence?* They got a team?"

"Steph, I thought you was going to Syracuse? Now you going to Georgia Tech? We all know Coach Bobby Cremins came and landed the jet in Coney Island in the middle of the night! He came to the projects and *kidnapped* your ass!"

I never laughed harder in my life than that '95 McDonald's weekend. It was like an instant brotherhood. We were all from different places all over the country—Chicago, Detroit, Denver, Inglewood—and we were all that one-in-a-million story. That one kid in our hood who actually made it out. It was a beautiful moment.

Naturally, with me and Steph being from New York, we were the leaders of the group. That's just how it is, man. I don't make the rules. I got receipts for that too. I never exaggerate. Watch the footage. Every time clips from that game come up on social media, everybody always asks, "Yo, why does KG and Vince and Chauncey and all these dudes on both teams got Band-Aids over their ears?"

It's one of those little unsolved mysteries in basketball culture. What happened was, we were out the day before the game seeing the Arch and visiting the children's hospital, and at the end of the day, all the guys were like, "Yo, what we doing tonight?"

So I said, "I'm going to get my ears pierced."

In '95, that was still kind of ahead of the curve. 2Pac had his ears pierced, and I was trying to look fly like Pac on national TV. So we all go to the mall that night. And this is when malls was *poppin'*. Picture it. KG, Paul, Chaunce, Tractor Traylor, and all these future legends outside the Sbarro's. Sippin' on the Orange

Julius. We all got on our McDonald's All-American sweatshirts and hats. That golden arch is looking like the Superman *S* on our chests. We're on top of the world, thinking we *made it*, son. We own this food court. Half the shorties were probably looking at us like, "Yo, do all these dudes work at Micky D's? They on their break or something?"

All the guys are coming up to me like, "Yo, you're really getting your ears pierced?"

I said, "Yeah."

"Alright, maybe I'll do it. My moms is gonna kill me. Does it *hurt*, dog?"

We go to one of them stores where teenage girls go to get their ears pierced before the dance, you feel me? They got up the boy-band posters on the walls. Backstreet Boys. Boyz II Men. Imagine KG walking up in that joint, barking out, "Ey, how much for *boff* ears? Do I get a discount?"

People were looking at us crazy. I got mine done, and then Steph got his done, and then *everybody* followed. New York always had that swag! We the trendsetters. I got the receipts! I remember Paul Pierce sitting in the chair when they came with the piercing gun, trying not to scream.

"I don't like needles, man! Shit!"

Little girls looking at him, shaking their heads like, *Come on, son*.

We all showed up to the gym the next day and the organizers shut it down quick. This was at the height of the East Coast/West Coast stuff. All the media hysteria about hip-hop. McDonald's wasn't about to put us on TV looking like Pac. They thought we were going to corrupt the youth. They made us all take our earrings out for the game, but the wounds hadn't healed up yet, so we had to put Band-Aids over the holes. We were all trying to look fly for the cameras and instead we looked crazy. But thankfully, the game itself was iconic. I remember KG asking me to show him some moves during the warm-ups, and I was teaching him some crossovers. The thing is, he was on the other team, so I said, "Yo, don't be using this on me in the game, alright?"

He used it on me in the game. I reached for the ball, and he pulled out my own trick on me.

Everybody was dying laughing on the bench.

I said, "Really, dog? *Really?* On national TV?"

He was talking *wild* shit, even back then. KG was exactly who you thought he was, even at seventeen. He was born KG. It wasn't an act. Dude had 18 points, 11 rebounds, 4 assists, and 3 blocks in 22 minutes.

The West beat us 126–115, but we put on a show. I did my thing. A lot of people come up to me on the street to this day and they say that they were watching that game on TV that day, and I was doing things they'd never seen before with the basketball. At one point, the announcer said, "Shammgod with the ball. The greatest handle since the *Messiah*."

I tell people all the time: If my name was Steve, or Jimmy, would I be remembered in the same way? Probably not. But my name is my name, and my game is my game. From that day on, "Shammgod" was more than just a person. It was a culture. If you were dribbling the ball up the court between your legs, you were doing "a Shammgod." If you were putting the ball behind your back and then between your legs and making the whole defense spin out of orbit, you were doing "a Shammgod." If you were showing up to the park in Tims and jeans and still crossing up motherfuckers for fun, you were doing "a Shammgod."

I didn't even realize what a big deal it was at the time. I was just a kid having the time of my life. Eating steak and shrimp. Smiling for the cameras. Doing my thing live on CBS. The best part was that I knew my mom was in the crowd watching me. I always wanted to be her hero as much as she was my hero. I felt like I was trying to save both of our lives, you feel me? Everything I was doing before my son was born, I was doing for her. For *us*. Just to try to get us a better life. I used to always imagine that she was in the crowd watching me, whether I was all alone at the park or I was playing in a high school game. My imagination was so good that it really felt like she was there, even though she wasn't physically there. I could feel her presence and her love, and I'd always go home and tell her everything that happened in the game.

But that night, she was there to see it with her own eyes. She was really, finally there.

I remember going up to her after the game, like, "Ma, did I do good? What did you think?"

She had tears in her eyes and she said, "Oh my God, you are *amazing*. I can't believe what you do with that basketball. How do you put it between your legs like that?"

"Practice, Ma. Practice."

The craziest part was that when you made the McDonald's All-American squad they literally gave you a gold card for a year's supply of Micky D's for free. Imagine giving that to a seventeen-year-old kid. It was like having the Platinum AmEx. I came back to Harlem like the Black Santa Claus. I would pull up to the McDonald's on 125th after playing at the park with fifteen of my boys, sixteen of my homegirls.

"Yo, gimmie seventeen orders of McNuggets, please."

I'm pulling up with the whole *block*.

"What you want? What you want? It's Christmas, young money. Get yourself a ten-piece. Everything's on Shamm."

We had the fry cooks working overtime.

"Gimmie twelve quarter-pounders, B. And you know what? Lemme get a milk shake. Don't be telling me the ice cream machine is broken, sir. I'm an *All-American*. I'mma be dunking my french fries in that vanilla shake. Put it all on the gold card, B."

Free-ninety-nine.

Some nights, we had the whole hood up in there. I'm pulling up with a whole third-grade *class*, like we're on a field trip. What they gonna do anyway? Call Ronald McDonald on me?

You know how good it feels to give a ten-year-old kid a free Big Mac who ain't never had one in his life? Those kids would be looking at me like I was bigger than MJ.

My biggest dream when I was their age was to be able to breathe easy. To feel safe. I didn't care what I had to do to make that happen. Whether I was a ball player or I worked at the cable company, I just wanted to not worry about where my next meal was coming from. If you grow up with that feeling, it never really leaves you.

I've been fortunate enough to travel all around the world, all because I'm good at dribbling a basketball. I've eaten thousand-dollar dinners. I've driven in cars worth half a mil. I've had caviar in Russia. I've had Peking duck in China. I've been to Michelin-star restaurants. But let me tell you something, B. And this is a fact.

Nothing I've ever tasted in my life was as good as that first bite of a free McNugget, just sitting in the 125th Street McDonald's in Harlem, surrounded by my people, knowing that I did exactly what I said I was gonna do. I was an *All-American*.

That was the best thing I ever tasted.

The summer right before I left for college, me and Mase had a fight that cut right to the soul. We were playing ball in the park, like usual. But for some reason, nobody else was around, and we were playing one-on-one. Mase could really ball, by the way. Don't get it twisted. When I tell you him and Cam were *nice*, I'm not being charitable. They played together on the same team at Manhattan Center High, and they went all the way to the city championship game. Now, they weren't as nice as *me*. But they were nice, you feel me? Mase was just good enough to be talking wild trash to me all the time whenever we played.

"Come on, Shamm. I showed you this game. I taught you everything you know."

Sometimes it's the people closest to you who just know how to get on your nerves the most, right? We never really fought, but we were at that age where everybody is about to go their separate ways, and you could kind of feel that tension in the air. I was about to go to Providence. Cam was about to go to play junior college ball in Texas. Mase was about to go to play at SUNY Purchase, but that was never his real dream. He always wanted to be a rapper. But at that time, how do you become a rapper? It wasn't like you could just start recording into your iPhone and put it up on SoundCloud. You had to get into a real studio, in a real booth, with a real producer. You had to have either connections or money, and we didn't have neither. So we did it the old-fashioned way. I would take Mase to all my high school games, and he'd just start freestyling for the crowd during warm-ups. After the game, we'd go back to Harlem and he'd post up on 139th and Lenox on the "rapper's corner" and just freestyle for anybody who was passing by. Him and Big L would be out there sometimes rapping for the pigeons, man. Nobody around, still going hard. There was a chicken joint right on the corner there, and they'd be rapping for the line of people waiting on their wings—in the rain, in the sleet, in the snow. If you been in line at that twenty-four-hour chicken spot at two o'clock in the morning, there's a good chance you heard Jay-Z or Nas or Fat Joe freestyling and you didn't even know it, because they weren't famous yet.

By that summer of '95, Mase was grinding, trying to get noticed, but he still didn't have a record deal. So we're playing this game of one-on-one at the park, and I guess I must've woke up on the wrong side of the bed that morning, because I was talking trash. I picked the wrong battle, because Mase is never gonna back down. Everything just starts escalating, like it does when you're seventeen. It starts getting personal. Now we're not even playing ball no more, we're just arguing about *everything*.

For some reason, I said, "Man, you're always talking about rapping, rapping, rapping. You ain't no rapper. You think you're gonna be Biggie? You ain't never gonna be Big."

That cut him deep. As soon as I said it, I thought: *Oop.*

Mase looked at me and he said, "Oh, you think you're gonna be a ball player? You going to the League, huh? You think you Isiah Thomas? You ain't Isiah. You're never gonna be nothing. You'll be out here at this park next year."

That cut me deep.

We're both just looking at each other like: *Yo. Damn. Really?*

You know when you get into it with your boy and you're both just sitting there steaming for like five minutes, just shaking your head, not saying anything? It was like that. Then, I don't know who said it. I wish it was me, but it was probably him. But one of us said. "Alright. Cool. If you're the one who makes it out first, I'll be the first one riding with you."

"Cool."

"Cool."

"Let's get a ten-piece."

Within two years, I was in the NBA. Mase was rapping with Biggie. But hold on. I'm getting ahead of myself. We weren't shit yet. Yes, I had a scholarship. But I'm not going to lie to you—Providence was not the first college on my list. Like everything in my life, it's a crazy story how I ended up there. Of course, I always wanted to go to Georgia Tech with Steph. But college ball ain't McDonald's. They were never going to take two point guards from the same year in the same city. I was always the backup choice in case Steph decided not to go to Georgia Tech. Their coach, Bobby Cremins, told me right to my face, "We're waiting on Steph."

So then I started talking to Syracuse. I loved watching Pearl Washington on my old VHS tapes, and he went to 'Cuse, so that was my second choice. Their coach was a young Jim Boheim. He told me to my face, "Shamm, we love you. But we're waiting on Steph."

I said, "You're waiting on Steph? I just talked to Steph. He's going to Georgia Tech."

He said, "We feel confident. We're waiting on Steph."

I thought: *Bro, do you know how cold it is up here? Steph ain't coming to 'Cuse.*

He said, "You can come if you want. We'd love to have you, but you'd have to play behind Steph."

Nah. Forget it, sir. But at least he was honest with me. Not all coaches are straight with you. That's why I don't begrudge any of these college players moving around now in the transfer portal, and getting their money, because 95 percent of these college coaches are looking at you like you're a 2K player. You're not a human being. You're not a seventeen-year-old kid moving your whole life up to a new town. You're just an asset to them. They slick. They smiling. They telling you everything you want to hear. But they're looking out for *them.*

Boheim wanted Steph. That was his trophy. And Steph was *never* going up there. A couple weeks later, I signed with Providence. The very same day, Steph signed with Georgia Tech. Boheim must have been fuming. Now he had zero guards.

The first time we played Syracuse in the Big East, I had 18 points and 12 assists, and the whole game I was looking over at their bench, doing the MJ shrug to Boheim, like: *See what could've been?*

But again, I'm getting ahead of myself. It's a habit. How does a Harlem kid end up in Providence, Rhode Island, anyway?

Fate, brother.

Years before graduating from high school, I hopped a turnstile and got locked up. I was fifteen years old. I was at the 145th Street station. I had to go downtown to 42nd Street to catch the F to go to school. I was late, and I could hear the train coming, so I ran down the steps and I leaped right over the turnstile. I see the open doors of the subway car, and they're just about to close, and I'm almost there . . . And right as I'm about to step through the gap—*yoink.*

I get pulled back. I got snatched up by two NYPD subway cops.

I remember the first thing I said was, "My moms can't know, my moms can't know, my moms can't know."

I just kept repeating that.

"Take me in, make me pay the fine, do whatever you gotta do. But don't tell my moms."

Did you know they got a little subway jail? For real. Right in the station. There's a little lockup down there. I'm handcuffed, and they're taking me in, and this dude Bobby Gonzalez saw what was happening. He knew me from AAU ball. He was a famous high school coach in the Bronx and Harlem. He just happened to be walking through the station when he saw them taking me in, and he said, "Hold on, what's going on? I know this kid."

They said, "He hopped the turnstile. We gotta take him in."

Bobby said, "He's a good kid. I'll pay whatever. I'll sign whatever. Just let him go to school."

The cops were like, "You can vouch for this kid?"

He said, "Yes, a hundred percent."

They let me go. Bobby could've just kept walking that day. He didn't really know me like that. But he went out of his way to help me, and from that day on we became really close. He ended up going up to Providence to be an assistant coach, and I never forgot what he did for me. They were one of the first schools to really recruit me seriously, and once I knew it wasn't going to work out with Georgia Tech and Syracuse, I thought: *You know what? Providence. Big East. I'll get minutes. I can run the show. Bobby is up there. I can drive back down to the city and see my son. Why not?*

When I committed, I told Bobby: "Yo, remember when you bailed me out of subway jail?"

So that's how I wound up at Providence. Shenanigans, son. It's funny how life works out. If you don't think God's talking to you all the time, you ain't listening hard enough.

(And by the way, if you really want to know how deep the butterfly effect goes, think about this: Not only did I end up at Providence because Steph didn't go to Syracuse, but Jason Williams, aka White Chocolate, was supposed to go to *Providence* originally, but since I ended up there, he ended up switching to Marshall, and then eventually to Florida. Can you imagine Shammgod and

White Chocolate on the same squad? Two of the most creative dribblers to ever do it. We'd have had the whole Big East on roller skates. Our games would've come with the parental advisory warning, son.)

Anyway. There I go again. Daydreaming. Stay with me. It's fall 1995. The Harlem kid is a college boy now. It's freshman registration. The leaves are turning orange up in Rhode Island. The shorties got on their college sweatshirts. Everything is new to me. Remember when the Fresh Prince went to UCLA in the later seasons? That was me. I was just taking it all in. But we got a problem. Now, I know I said that I never lie to you. But I did withhold some information in this little story of ours. Nothing wrong with that. It was for narrative purposes, you feel me? In New York City, we don't tell stories in a straight line. You gotta just roll with it. See, at that point in time, when I was going into my freshman year, my name was not God Shammgod. Not really.

If you looked in a newspaper from that time, there was no God Shammgod on the stat sheet.

There was only Shammgod Wells.

See, when I was little, nobody had a problem with the name God Shammgod at PS92. That name don't really raise eyebrows in Harlem or the Bronx. We got all kinds of interesting names. But when I started going downtown to a nice Catholic high school, the nuns were *bugging*.

"Your name is *what*, son?"

"God."

They were crossing themselves. Looking up to the heavens.

"Oh my Lord. We're not calling you that in this classroom."

One of the nuns flipped the letters and started calling me Dog Shammgod. Can you believe that? In New York City, our nuns are a different breed. They *wilin'*. "Dog Shammgod, please report to the front of the class."

Finally, she couldn't take it anymore.

"Alright, what's your middle name, son?"

"It's complicated."

"What is it?"

"Ain't got one."

"Well, what's your mother's last name?"

"Wells."

"Then from now on, you're Shammgod Wells. Please take a seat, Mr. Wells."

That was it. From that day on, I was Shammgod Wells. All through high school, all the headlines in the paper would be "Shammgod Wells Scores 40." But I never legally changed my name. I thought whatever you wrote on that math quiz was your name. So I show up to freshman registration at Providence, and we have to fill out all this stuff for the NCAA. We had to bring our birth certificate and everything. Out of the blue, my coaches are like, "Hey, we got a problem. The registration office is saying your name doesn't match."

I said, "Oh, word? Yeah, my real name is God Shammgod, but the nuns never wanted to call me that."

They were looking at me like I was an alien.

"Say what?"

"My real name. God Shammgod. Like my daddy. But I always use Wells, like my mother."

"Well then we got a problem, son. We can't put Wells on an NCAA roster unless that's your legal name."

"Alright, cool. How much does it cost to change it?"

"Five hundred dollars."

"Five hundred!"

"Five hundred."

In my head, I'm doing the mental math of how many pairs of Jordans I can buy with five hundred dollars. I had no idea how important that decision was, but in the moment, with the pen in my hand, I decided to just stick with God Shammgod. It turned out to be the best five hundred I never spent. But at first, it was actually mad confusing for people, because I was an All-American as Shammgod Wells, and now I'm coming into the Big East as this mythical God Shammgod character. I was Metta World Peace before Metta World Peace, you feel me? I was the artist formerly known as Prince. People didn't understand how to take it. They thought I had purposely changed my name to "God." They instantly thought I was cocky or crazy or *something*. How can I even explain?

"God? You think you're a God or something?"

"Homie, it was an *administrative mix-up*."

That don't sound cool. So I just rolled with it. If somebody pressed me on it, I'd just say, "Yo, ask my father. That's my namesake."

What I never explained to anyone is the deeper meaning behind my full name. It means "a savior to thyself, one who was worthy of greatness."

When I really think about it, that's the path I've been on my whole life.

Okay, so picture it: A black kid from Harlem named God Shammgod, dropped into a college campus in suburban Rhode Island in 1995. It was a culture shock, I'm not gonna lie to you. The homies was out there listening to Nirvana, man. The home-girls was out there listening to *Seal*. What was that band with the one black dude and the five white dudes with the harmonicas and shit? They was out there listening to *Hootie and the Blowfish*, son. I came from the corner with Big L and Mase and Cam and Biggie and DMX barkin' at strangers, and these dudes are at the dorm party drinking white wine, trying to play Boyz II Men for the shorties. *Soft.* I was in another world now. Another galaxy. And mind you, I don't drink. I don't smoke. That blew the white homies' minds.

"Bro, you want a beer?"

"Nah, I don't drink."

"Bro, how do you talk to girls then?"

"Yo, I'm from Harlem. They come and talk to *me*."

I was an alien. They didn't know what to do with me. Thank God, I had my teammates. I had my sanctuary. I had basket-ball. On the court, I hit the ground running. I set the Big East freshman assist record with 182 dimes. I used to be driving the other student sections nuts. Imagine a freshman named God coming into your building and crossing up your All-American. I was like one of those old-school WWF bad guys when I went into those Big East gyms. I'd be coming out of the tunnel just laughing.

Boooooo!!! Booooooo!!! You SUCK!!!

I'd be smirking. Cracking my neck. I had 'em losing their minds.

I'll never forget, at the end of that first season, we were playing at Notre Dame, and I'd never been in an environment like that before. I mean, I'd been in gyms in the hoods where they were patting kids down coming in and out. Checking for paraphernalia, you feel me? I'd played at the Rucker in front of dudes strapped up with the *Call of Duty* arsenal. But at Notre Dame? In February 1996? Middle of winter in *Indiana*? Nothing else to do but be pissed off? And *God Shammgod* is coming into your house? Yo, I had these white boys going *crazy*.

Their whole student section had made signs.

"GOD??? YOU'RE THE DEVIL!!!"

"YOU'RE GOING TO HELL #12"

"THOU SHALT NOT STEAL"

It was out of control. They were all over me. I loved it. I dropped 10 and 10 on them and we won at the buzzer. I walked out of that gym just smiling at everybody. You just gotta smile through the hate sometimes.

"Take care, y'all. Talk to God. I'll pray for you."

I had Dick Vitale screaming out my name. Everybody in the hood loved Dickie V. That's how you knew you really made it, when Dickie was losing his mind, screaming out, "Shammgod! The Diaper Dandy! He's *awesome*, baybee!"

I had dudes calling me up from Harlem, talking about, "Yo, did you hear what Dickie V was saying about you? He shouted you out, dog."

Two weeks later, Allen Iverson and Georgetown came into our building, and that was like the Hood Super Bowl that year, you feel me? I don't care who you ask—if you talk to somebody who knows basketball, and you talk about the crossover, you're gonna hear two names: Shammgod and Iverson.

We were the two best to ever do it. That's facts.

Now, AI, that's my *guy*. I love that man. But at that time, we were like two samurais from rival clans, you feel me? AI was from Hampton Roads, Virginia, and they didn't play down there. They had some real gangsters in those streets. Real killers. Real OGs. His people and my people, they were in the same orbit, you know what I mean? I might've played in one or two off-the-books money games in Hampton Roads as a kid. Me and AI, we were representing more than just Providence and Georgetown. We were representing our neighborhoods. He had his boys coming up from Virginia. I had my boys coming up from Harlem. Like I said: Hood Super Bowl. So the night before that game, I was getting myself so *hype* in our dorm room. My roommate was my boy Jamel Thomas, and he was a Brooklyn kid. When you go to war, what do you do? You put your Tims on. So I literally had my Tims on, and I'm stomping around the room, listening to Pac.

I'm screaming out:

"'All Eyez on Me'! 'All Eyez on Me'!"

People are trying to do their math homework, dog. They're banging on the door:

"Hey! Hey! Excuse me!"

"Motherfuckin' OG! 'All Eyez on Me'!"

We're gassing each other up.

"Tomorrow, B! Tomorrow! We doing this shit for NEW YORK *CITY*!"

We're blasting Pac, and we got on the VHS tape of Pearl Washington playing against the famous Georgetown full-court press. See, the whole week, my teammates were all nervous, talking about, "You know what John Thompson is gonna do. He's gonna try to press you, Shamm. You better be ready for that pressure."

So now I'm stomping around the dorm room, barking like DMX.

Jamel is doing the callbacks, like we rapping:

"Pressure? They talking about *pressure*, son? Do they know where we from?!"

"(Harlem!)"

"Pressure, son? Really?"

"(Brooklyn! Real niggas!)"

"I'm not even wearing my Nikes tomorrow, B!! I'm balling in TIMS!!! I'm ready for war!!!"

"(Never scared!!!)"

I think we slept like three hours that night. We're at the game the next day, and AI pulled up with his whole *block*. We pulled up with half of Harlem and half of Brooklyn. It was like a high school game. This is a Big East basketball game on ESPN2. And you got killers standing around looking like we on 139th Street. The energy was crazy. So we get in the layup line, and we're just getting loose, and all of a sudden I hear this voice behind me.

"Son, they shook. Scared to death, scared to look . . ."

I ignore it. I shoot my layup. Go back into the line.

I hear it again. Louder this time. Is dude talking to me? Nah, motherfucker is *rapping* at me. I turn around, and I see AI staring me straight in my face, singing Mobb Deep.

Son, they shook
'Cause ain't no such things as halfway crooks
Scared to death, scared to look, they shook

Hahahaha. Yo!! What? I'm just staring back at him wild-eyed, my veins popping out. We're nose-to-nose. You remember back in the day when Hulk Hogan took on the Ultimate Warrior? The unstoppable force versus the immovable object.

He's thinking: *I'm about to* kill *your ass for Virginia.*

I'm thinking: *I'm about to* kill *your ass for Harlem.*

That's my man. We put on a show for everybody. We actually ended up beating them that night by like twenty, but nobody remembers that game for what happened on the court. Everybody remembers it because my crazy-ass teammate Jamel Thomas almost started a *riot* because he threw AI into the stands at the end of the game. There was a big fight, and the refs and security were separating everybody, and every time I ever run into AI now, he reminds me of what I was screaming at him and his boys, and he's crying laughing . . .

Obviously, he had his controversy in high school when he got into a fight at the bowling alley, and so allegedly—I black out when I talk shit—but allegedly, according to AI, once I had enough security guards between me and his boys, I was screaming, "You ain't never been to no real jail! You was in juvy! You ain't no real killers! You was in baby jail!"

Hahahaha. I was out of my mind. AI, that's my *guy*. We had the ultimate respect for each other, and that's exactly why we were trying to *murder* one another every time we got on the court. Two samurais, man. Another kindred spirit that God put into my life. Another *one of one*.

We finished my freshman season 18–12, and we just missed out on March Madness. But I'd done what I came there to do. I made a name for myself (again). I put God Shammgod on the map. I played in the Big East tournament at Madison Square Garden in front of my son and my family and all my boys. I had Dickie V going nuts. I battled with Iverson. I made everybody proud. I was going back to Harlem that summer as a hero.

Summer '96. Let's go. I couldn't wait to just chill at the park with Mase and Cam and all my boys. Barbecues. Block parties. *Real* music. *Real* shorties. Home. The way it always was, and the way it always will be, you know what I mean? That's the irony of the hood. That's what is really hard to explain to outsiders. The hood is something you always dream about escaping, and then when you finally escape it, you always dream about going back.

So I come home from school for the summer, and after I see my son, the first thing I do is go to the park, and I'm catching up with everybody, and it's all "Yo, what was it like playing in the Garden? You meet Iverson? Is he cool? You going to the league next year?"

Then I hear this car coming down the block before I even see it. Base rattling. Engine revving. It sounded like a million dollars. This silver BMW 318 pulls up real slow. Brand-new. The windows roll down, and the first thing I see is the three-thousand-dollar Virgin Mary chain. It's sparkling like a cartoon. *Bling, bling, bling, bling.* It's so icy it's radiating a holy aura. Who the hell is crazy enough to rock a Virgin Mary chain on 140th Street? Dude is smiling ear to ear. I've been seeing that smile since I was nine years old.

"Peace, God. What's good? You ready to ride with me?"

It was Mason Betha. My first friend. But he wasn't Mason Betha no more. He had transformed.

He was the thing he always dreamed of being.

He was Ma$e.

Cue his music, man.

What you know about going out?
Head west, red Lex, TVs all up in the headrest

In one summer, everything was about to change. It was *on* now.

While I was away at Providence my freshman year, Mase was doing everything in his power to become a rapper. He had dropped out of SUNY Purchase after a few months and was back in Harlem, trying to get into any studio he could and record some tracks. But mostly he was just rapping for anybody who would listen. His mother told him that if he wasn't going to school, he couldn't stay at the house, so he was just couch surfing, sleeping on floors, waiting on a miracle. It's crazy how God puts certain people in your life exactly when you need them. He put Mase into my life when I needed a friend. He put Tiny Archibald into my life when I needed a mentor. He put Kevin Jackson into my life when I needed a master sensei.

For Mase, that person was this dude named Cooda. How can I even explain Cooda to you if you're not from the hood? Cooda was just *one of them dudes*, you feel me? Everybody knows *one of them dudes*. Nobody even knew where this dude came from or when he showed up in Harlem. He wasn't from New York. But one day, he just showed up and all of a sudden, everybody knew

Cooda. Even if you weren't cool with him, you'd be like, "Yeah, I'm cool with Cooda. He aight."

To put it in perspective for you, he always had two homeboys with him named Black Fred and Meat.

Now you getting the picture? *Hustler*. Hustler with a heart of gold.

Everybody in the hood says they're a hustler. But this dude Cooda could really get it out the mud. He could get you anything. He could find a way to make a dollar out of fifty cents. He got real cool with Biggie before he really blew up, and he ended up being his road manager, taking him around the country to rap in these tiny clubs for five thousand bucks or whatever. Cooda was always looking out for the dudes who hadn't been put on yet. He started messing with Mase's sister's best friend, and one day, Mase's sister was like, "You think Biggie can rap? You know who can *really* rap?"

"Who? Big L?"

"Nah, my brother."

"Come on."

"No, I'm telling you, he can *really* rap."

"Ain't he like fourteen?"

"No, he's eighteen. I'm telling you . . . Hang on, lemme get his mixtape."

Cooda listened to the mixtape, and he was blown away. His gears started turning. He's scheming. He said, "Alright, gimme two weeks."

Two weeks go by, and Cooda comes to Mase. He says, "Alright, you wanna be a rapper? I need you to be outside the

Apollo Theater tomorrow night. I got somebody who wants to hear you."

"Damn . . . The Apollo?"

"Yeah, but we not going in. Just post up on the corner around ten. Don't be late. And try to look fly."

So Mase goes and stands outside the Apollo. And he waits under that famous red neon sign. We'd seen it a million times. They used to record *Showtime at the Apollo* in that joint, and we'd watch it on TV. It was ten blocks from where we lived, but we had literally never even been inside. It was right there, but it was another world, you feel me?

So he's waiting, and he's waiting . . . It's the middle of winter, freezing cold. He's got on his best Tommy Hilfiger rain jacket and a Nautica snowcap. Plus some Tims that he borrowed from Cam. He's freezing to death, and the crowd is coming out from the show. Hours go by. No Cooda. No nobody. He's shivering. Now it's midnight, and he's wondering if Cooda was just playing him. That's what you get for getting your hopes up in the hood. *Stupid. This dude don't know nobody . . .*

All of a sudden, a dark green Land Cruiser pulls up on the sidewalk. The window rolls down. Big homie is sitting in the driver's seat. *Bigger* homie is sitting in the passenger's seat with dark shades on. Music is blasting out of the system. Bass thumping. Reefer pouring out the windows.

Then that unmistakable voice rings out.

"*Yow sunn.* I heard you rap."

It's the Notorious BIG.

"Yeah, I rap."

"So let's hear it. Come around the other side."

Mase runs to the passenger's side, and Big rolls the window down.

"Let's hear it, Shorty."

Mase had one shot to change his life. Thirty seconds. No mic. Freezing cold. Shivering. Standing on the sidewalk. Staring a legend straight in the face.

So what did he do?

Mase did what Mase does. He rapped his ass off.

When he was done, Big turned to the driver.

He said, "Yo, I like Shorty."

That was it. Big rolled the window up, and they drove off. Mase didn't know it, but he had changed his life forever. Big's word was gold. He started telling everybody that the little shorty from Harlem could really rap. Big started telling Cooda to bring Mase around whenever he had shows in New York. He would be sitting backstage at Big's shows, telling all the homegirls, "Y'all don't know me yet, but in a couple of months, I'm gonna be the biggest thing in rap. Y'all are gonna know Ma$e."

They were rolling their eyes, like, *Alright, shorty. You someone's little brother or something?*

A few months later, Cooda and Mase went down to this big rap convention in Atlanta. At that time, Mase was sleeping on the floor in Cooda's apartment. They didn't have any money for plane tickets, but economy seats were cheaper than the gas it would've taken to drive down to Atlanta and back, so Cooda sold his Acura. They had one shot. They had to hustle and get in front of the right producer. Cooda found out from Big that Puff Daddy and Bad Boy were putting on a party at the Hard Rock Cafe. So they showed up at the Hard Rock, but their name wasn't on the list. Cooda is out there hustling the bouncers, talking about "Come on man, I know Big. I know Puff."

The bouncers weren't hearing it. Jermaine Dupri is walking in, Kris Kross is walking in. Cameras are flashing. Shorties are going crazy, asking for autographs. And Cooda and Mase are just standing on the sidewalk, getting pushed back by security. Everybody in life has had that moment, right? Just that gut-punch moment. When you feel like you ain't worth anything to the world. When somebody is yelling at you, "Yo, get back, shorty. You not on the list."

And right at that moment, when Mase had spent his last hundred dollars on a Versace shirt to stand outside a Hard Rock Cafe and try to get noticed, God intervened. I don't know how else you can explain it. Puff's manager noticed Cooda in the crowd, and he got them in. Then there was *another* barricade with two other mean-looking bouncers around the VIP, and Cooda was able to get Puff's attention. The music was so loud that nobody could hear, but Cooda was pointing at Mase and just saying "Big."

Puff pulled them into the VIP.

"Yo, it's Biggie's boy."

"Huh?"

"Big. Big says he's *nice*."

"Shorty right here?"

"Yeah, shorty right here."

So Puff stopped the music. He told the DJ to put on a beat. And then he handed Mase the mic, right there in the middle of the club, with Jermaine Dupri and Kris Kross and a thousand shorties watching.

He said, "Shorty, I'm gonna give you one chance. Don't play yourself."

And Mase did what Mase does. With everything on the line, with no warning, five minutes after standing out on the corner in front of the Hard Rock, he rapped his ass off.

Puff started dancing. Everybody started dancing. They went crazy for the kid. In the blink of an eye, Mason Betha became Ma$e.

After that, it was a wrap.

By the time Mase got back to New York, he had a record deal waiting from Bad Boy. Now, obviously a lot has transpired with Puff and Bad Boy in the three decades that have gone by. As I'm writing this, the details are still coming out, and everything still has to play out in the courts. I can't speak on it, not because I'm scared of speaking on it, but because I can only tell you my story through my eyes, as I lived it. Mase and Puff, that's Mase's story to tell. All I can tell you is that in 1996, Puff was the hottest king-maker in music, and getting a deal with Bad Boy to be the num-ber two to Big was beyond any kid's wildest dreams. Going from sleeping on the floor and rapping on street corners to a deal with Bad Boy? In a snap of a finger? It doesn't get any wilder.

I remember Bad Boy gave Mase a $50,000 advance for sign-ing. They slid him a check across the table on a Friday, and Mase ran to the first bank he saw in Harlem. He never had a bank account in his life, but they let him take out $25,000 in cash for that weekend. Him and Cooda went to the mall, and by the end of that weekend, he needed the *other* twenty-five grand. He got to play Harlem Santa Claus for his mother and his sister and everybody. He made sure everybody was eating good. Everybody and their cousin had the extra warm hoodie, you know what I mean?

He made it. I'd say it was a miracle, but he did it all himself. With no help, and no connections, Mase blew *himself* up.

By the time I came back home from Providence for summer vacation, he was pulling up in the BMW 318. He was in the studio with Big. He was going out on the road and playing shows. He was doing his thing. But the thing you have to remember about 1996 is that there was *music*, and then there was *BET*. And then there was *MTV*. Before YouTube and social media, music videos were everything. I can't even make a kid today understand what it was like to be chilling with your boys sitting around the TV and all of a sudden Aaliyah's "Rock the Boat" music video comes on. That was a seminal moment, son. Everybody stopped. You couldn't pause it and play it back right away. You might only see that video once a day. So your homeboys would be yelling out to you in the kitchen, "Yo! Yo, yo, yo, yo, yoooooooo! It's on, son! It's on!"

You'd come into the Good Room *sprinting*.

Music videos *were* the culture in '96. And there was a hierarchy. If you got on BET, you were famous in the hood. But if you got some play on MTV, you were famous on another level. But see, we didn't even know that at the time. We didn't get it, because we weren't watching MTV. Then one day late that summer, me and Mase take a drive up to the Palisades Mall in West Nyack, New

York. For people who don't know New York, this is the *nice* mall. When we were growing up, I didn't even know places like this existed. I'd never been there, because you had to have real money to go out there. But now Mase finally got his record deal, and I'm at Providence doing my thing with a little bit of money in my pocket (what the NCAA don't know won't hurt 'em). So we're not just going shoppin'. We're going *choppin'*, son. We got bands now. We're gonna go see what's going on in the Foot Locker. We up in *Macy's* now, son. You know you got money when you come out a store smelling like free cologne.

Man, listen . . .

We park, and we get up into the food court, and everything is chill. Then I notice this one older white lady is looking at us. Okay, nothing new. We don't want no problems. We're chilling. But then she creeps up on us, and she's like, "Ohmygosh, hi. I'm so sorry for bothering you, but can I get an autograph?"

She's looking at Mase, of course. Not me.

I had never even seen somebody sign an autograph before. Not in person. We don't do that in the hood. I'm looking at the lady like: *Yo, you know he's not a baseball player, right?*

Mase is looking around, all nervous, and he's like, "Alright, cool. Cool. But calm down."

I'm thinking: *Yo, why's he telling her to chill?*

All of a sudden, it's like a text message got sent to every shorty in the mall. You just see all these heads turning toward us. People are looking up from their burgers, prairie-doggin'. Then there was like a murmur. And Mase is signing this autograph superfast, like, "Alright, cool. Have a good one."

He turns to me like, "Yo, we gotta go."

"We gotta go? What?"

All of a sudden, everything popped off. Hysteria. I see a group of eighteen shorties—a *gaggle* of white shorties—and they're running up the escalator, screaming out, "Mase!!! Mase!!! Ahhh-hhh!!! Oh myyyyy gosssshh!!!"

Mase takes off. Whoosh. He's running. Shit! Now I'm running. I don't even know what's happening, but we're running through this mall, and then as we're running, more people are looking, and the gaggle of shorties just keeps getting bigger and bigger—and now we got what must be 150 shorties chasing us, *screaming*, and I'm talking *screaming*. I feel like girls don't even scream like that now, like they did back in the day.

I'm literally beside myself, like, *Yo, what is going on? Why are they chasing us?*

What I didn't realize was that the video for 112's "Only You" had just come out. It was an R&B joint, but on the remix, they had Mase and Biggie rapping on it. They started playing that joint on MTV around the clock, and Mase is in the video with his baby face and his red biker jacket in Times Square, looking all *cute*, so he had these suburban girls in a full-on panic. They was having a conniption. It was black Beatlemania. We got trapped, and we ran into a store and they literally had to roll down the security gate to keep these girls out. Their hands were coming through the grate and they were screaming, and I'm looking at Mase shaking my head like, "Yo, you turned this place into the *zombie apocalypse*, son! We gonna die!"

Survived nineteen years in the hood just to get taken out in West Nyack. *Damn.*

But thankfully, security got us up out of there. We went out through the loading dock, ran out to the whip. We drove back to Harlem feeling like superheroes. The cops actually told Mase that the next time he came to the mall, he had to call ahead of time and warn them; otherwise they were going to charge him with inciting a riot.

It's a funny thing when your boy blows up like that, because you're looking at him and laughing, just thinking back like, *Man, if only those girls knew . . . Six months ago, we was splitting one fried rice and a grape drink between four dudes outside the Chinese joint. Now you "Ma$e."*

My boy blew up.

Six months later, I blew up too. I had my MTV moment.

I did a move I'd done a hundred times in the hood. A defender was in front of me, and I crossed him up. I put his ass on skates. But I just so happened to do it on national television. And it just so happened, for reasons that I still can't understand, to blow everybody's mind. It doesn't matter if I run into a fourteen-year-old kid in Harlem, or I run into Steph Curry before a game, or I run into a Saudi prince. For the last damn near thirty years, anywhere I go all over the world—China, Saudi Arabia, South Africa, Nebraska—everybody asks me the same question. They all wanna know.

"How did you do that? Was it magic?"

Well . . .

This is the thing about magic: if you're looking at the hands, you're missing the trick. Ask any magician. Ask any street hustler. Any pickpocket. They always want your attention drawn to their hands, because the hands are not where it's all happening. The hands *are* the illusion. Dribbling is no different. You're not manipulating people's bodies. You're manipulating their mind. You're playing with their emotions.

If I cross you up—mean if I *really* cross you up, where you're falling backwards on your ass—I didn't cross you up; I'm not capable of that. You crossed *yourself* up. You *played* yourself.

Think on that. Let it marinate. Because we're going to come back to it.

March Madness 1997. My sophomore year. Up until that point, I didn't have any thoughts of going to the NBA. I was just focused on what was in front of me. When we made the tournament, I was just excited to do my thing in front of a big national audience. I had played in the Big East tournament on CBS, but March Madness is on a whole other level. Especially back then in '97, when most people just had like thirty channels max. It was like the whole world stopped for March Madness back in the day. We were the 10-seed. Nobody expects anything of the 10-seed. We were up against Marquette in the first round, and we knew them very well from the Big East. We *smoked* those boys. My boy Austin Croshere dropped 39 on them. He was going crazy. I actually didn't have that good a game—I dropped 6 points and had 8 assists. So when I found out that we had Duke in the next round, I was plotting my redemption.

I don't know what it is about playing certain schools. The Notre Dames and the Dukes of the world. For some reason, I always go off against those programs. Now, you have to remember, this wasn't just any Duke team. This was the Dukies squad who had Jeff Capel, Trajan Langdon, and Steve Wojciechowski. Remember Wojo? He was the original crazy-ass white boy. I loved that dude. I already knew Wojo really well because we had played against each other in camps when we were coming up. He was a year older than me, and he had made McDonald's All-American in '94, so I always looked at him with a lot of respect.

Now, what you have to understand about Wojo is that he was Charlie Hustle. He'd be diving all over the floor, mopping up loose balls, nipping at your heels, hand-checking you, talking wild trash without really cursing. Classic crazy-ass white boy. He was the perfect Coach K player, because he'd be so annoying that you'd forget all about what you were supposed to be doing. His job wasn't to score 30. It was to piss you off.

So right before the game, I remember my coach telling me, "Listen, you know what Wojo is about to do. He's going to come out and press you early. He's going to be slapping the floor and trying to bait you."

I'm like, "Yeah, whatever, Coach. I know Wojo. He's not going to be a problem. I ain't worried about that fake defense."

Jump ball. We win the tip. I got the ball at the point. National TV. March Madness. Bright lights. Full arena.

What's Wojo doing? He's slapping the floor, he's barking at me.

I lose my concentration for a second, because I'm almost trying not to laugh, and he rushes me. I was just a *split* second too slow to pull it back, and he poked it out. I got it back, but he was all over me again, and I was right by the sideline, and he slapped the ball right off my head and out of bounds. Duke ball. *Yo* . . .

Wojo turns around and he's *pushing* his own teammates, he's so hype. I turn to my coach, and he's looking at me fuming. I'm just laughing, like: *Alright. Chill. Chill. I got it. Don't worry about the little bulldog over there. Let me show these boys what Harlem is all about.*

Pssshhhh. Man, play my music.

Play 2Pac, "Hit 'Em Up." Can we get the rights to that? I don't care. Cue the movie montage. We were killing 'em. We had Coach K throwing his towel in frustration.

I hit a tough layup down the stretch with two defenders draped all over me for the *And-1*. The CBS announcer said the infamous line: "God getting it done on Sunday!"

Everybody quotes that all the time. But my favorite part was actually what he said after that: "When you grow up playing on the playgrounds of New York City, you *welcome* contact. You can't get on the court if you can't accept contact."

Truer words have never been spoken. That bucket broke their back, and we went on a big run to end the game. We ended up running them out of the gym by 30.

(Alright, I looked it up, and it was really only 11. But it damn sure felt like 30.)

Coach K came up to me after the game and said, "Son, I've never seen anyone dribble like you before."

That meant so much to me. A legend showing me respect like that. Because honestly, for so much of my life, so many coaches and scouts looked at my dribbling and thought it was "too much." They were always trying to rein me in. I remember my coach at Providence even started calling me "The Young and the Restless." Corny-ass nickname. But he was trying to humble me. To slow me down. During that March Madness, I just said, *Fuck it. I gotta be me.* I felt the energy from the crowds building and building, and I was playing ball like I was out in the park again. I was free.

I'll never forget, after the game, we were all sitting on the team bus waiting to go back to the hotel, and all of a sudden there was this commotion outside. Somebody was yelling. The bus was just about to pull out. But somebody was banging against the side of the bus: *Boooom, boooom, boooom, boooom.*

I'm like: *Yo, we about to have a problem? This happens in New York, you might have to start ducking under the seats.*

I'm looking at the driver, like: "Yo! Let's roll! They might start shooting!"

The driver opens the door. And who walks onto the bus but my boy Wojo. He's looking in the back. "Where's Shammgod?"

I'm like, "Yo! Wojo!"

He comes to the back of the bus, and I stand up like, "What's good?"

And he just says, "Heck of a game. Way to play."

And he gives me a big hug.

That's basketball, man. That's beautiful.

I remember he got off the bus and all my teammates were looking at me *crazy* like, "Yo, you know that crazy-ass white boy?"

I'm like, "Wojo? We go way back. That's the *homie*."

They were cracking up.

We went to Birmingham for the Sweet 16, and I went off against Tennessee-Chattanooga. I had 15-and-7 and the headline in the *Washington Post* said: PROVIDENCE GETS HELP FROM GOD.

They called my performance heavenly. That's when the hype really started to build a little bit. You could feel it in the interviews. We had Arizona in the Elite 8, and they had Mike Bibby and Michael Dickerson and Jason Terry. They were the heavy favorites, but I remember the media asking Bibby, "Providence is having this miracle run. What are you going to do to stop Shammgod?"

They had just beaten Kansas, and they shut down Jaques Vaughn, who was the No. 1 guard in the country. So Bibby was like, "We're not worried about Shammgod. We just played against Jacque Vaughn, and you see what we did against him."

We came up to the podium next, and they told me what Bibby said. And all my Harlem just came out of me, right there with the mic in my face.

I was like, "I don't care nothing about Jacque Vaughn. There's no one in the NCAA who can stop me. Definitely not them boys from Arizona."

Hahahaha. My coaches wanted to kill me. But it set the tone for us. We weren't going to be intimidated. I'll never forget, the first play of the game, we got the ball, and Mike Bibby picked me up full court. And I was just looking at him like, "Yo, you gotta be kidding me. There's *no way* this was Lute Olson's scouting report on me, dog. You think you're gonna press me? Do you know where I come from?"

I hit the first two jumpers, and I was looking at their bench like: *Yo, strap in. This is gonna be a long-ass night.*

They switched Michael Dickerson on me. The big man. And that was a big mistake. Everybody knows what happened next.

The move.

The crossover.

The "Shammgod."

But there's three really funny things about that moment that people don't understand.

First, this wasn't no exhibition game I did it in. This wasn't no Tuesday night nonconference warm-up game. Kids watch clips of it now, and they don't understand the context. This was in crunch time of the Elite 8. Arizona was up 9 with seven minutes left. We had to get a bucket. When I brought the ball up the court, there was nothing in my head. Everybody always asks me, "How did you plan out that move?"

I didn't plan *nothing*. When you're really in the flow of a game, you're not even in your own body. You're not thinking about what your hands are doing. You're just floating. You're like an artist. You're just creating, moment to moment. "The Shammgod" is not a move that I practiced the day before the game. It's not something I was planning out in warm-ups. It's my whole *life*, son. Every night I stayed up until two o'clock in the morning at the park, trying to shake my own shadow. Every morning I was ducking and weaving through the people in the subway with my basketball. Every time I was playing against five other dudes in my imagination, just trying to free up enough space to get a shot off. Every time I was playing at the Rucker against drug dealers and killers and I knew that the dudes sitting up in the bleachers had three *bands* riding on me. Every time I dribbled in the cold in the middle of winter until I couldn't even feel my hands anymore.

All of that went into that move.

I wasn't scared. I wasn't thinking. I was just free.

You can't describe the indescribable, but I'll try. What happened was, I was on the right wing, right at the top of the key. The big man came out on me, and I pulled a Jedi mind trick on him to make him think I was going to drive to my right. I actually *went* to my right. Physically, I went to the right. Only I didn't. See, I pushed the ball ahead of me, almost like I lost my handle. Except I *never* lose my handle. It was bait. As soon as the defender reached for it, I pulled it back in an instant and I went to my left.

Before your eyes could even process it, I was gone.

It broke the laws of physics.

What else would you call it, son? It was magic. It was "The Shammgod."

You know what the second funny part about it is? Man, this still kills me. But if you watch the tape back, the announcers didn't even react *at all*. They were talking about some nonsense, and I don't know if they were looking down at their notes or something, but the move happened so fast that they didn't even go crazy. For all the times the announcers have shouted out my name . . .

"The Friars are on Fire! Thanks to Shamm's divine guidance!"

"Shammgod with the almighty assist!"

"Shammgod rises again!"

This time, I pull out arguably the greatest crossover in basketball history, and it was *crickets*. But what's so cool about it is that they didn't need to say anything. The streets spoke for me. In living rooms all over America, from the hood to the suburbs, everybody was grabbing the arm of the couch, throwing the remote across the room, screaming out to their boys to come from the kitchen. You know in the movies when they show one house, and then they zoom out to a hundred houses, and then a thousand houses, and then the whole earth, all you hear is the echo coming out of every house, like:

*YYYYYYYYYYYYYYOOOOOOOOOOOOOOOooooooooooooooooo
oooooooooooooooooooooooooooooooooooooooooooooooooooooooooooooooooooo
oooooooo!!!!!!!!!!!!!!!*

Whole country was going bananas. But the TV broadcast acted like nothing happened.

Then the third funny thing? This is so depressing, man. But after all that, I got to the rim and I missed the layup. I blew it. I don't know what happened, but I *bricked* it. Thank God my boy Derrick Brown got the rebound off the glass and finished it.

So I really had no idea the magnitude of what had just happened.

I remember I was standing at the foul line for a free throw a minute later, and Dickerson looked at me and said, "Yo man, what the hell did you just do? That was crazy."

But I was so into the game that I remember just screaming at him, "Don't talk to me, son! Don't talk to me! None of y'all can fucking guard me!"

They ended up subbing Jason Terry into the game as their defensive stopper, and what you gotta understand is that JT is my *boy*. I love JT. But that day, I *murdered* JT. I think he came in and had four fouls in five minutes, and when they subbed him out of the game, I was so in my bag that I ran over to him and smacked him on the butt and said, "Yo, go *sit* your ass back down."

In my opinion, that was one of the greatest March Madness games of all time. There was so many twists and turns to it. There was so much emotion. We were down 85–78 with a minute left. Somehow we made it 85–85 and forced overtime. It was such a roller coaster that you had dudes crying on the bench when we got it to overtime. At the end of the day, we gave them everything we had, but they beat us 96–92.

I was so drained after the game that I didn't even understand what people were saying to me. I remember Jason Terry's father came up to me when I was coming out of the locker room, and everybody in basketball knows that JT's pops is a character. You know how he talks. He shook my hand and said, "Man, I've never seen anybody play basketball like you in my *liiiife*. In all my sixty-five years, I've never seen anything like it!"

(Years later, when I was with JT on the Mavericks, he was telling me how his pops would never shut up about that game, and we'd be cracking up doing the impression—"in my *liiiiiiife*.")

But in the moment, if I'm being honest with you, I was in a daze. I got to the podium with the media after the game, and they were asking me if I knew what I had done, and I didn't know what they were talking about. They were like, "Are you thinking about the NBA Draft?"

I'm like, "Draft? What?"

It didn't hit me until I went back to New York after the tournament to see my son. I was walking through the park in Harlem and little kids were screaming "Do the Shammgod, do the Shammgod."

But they weren't screaming out to me. They didn't even realize I was there. I was sitting on the gate, like I always did. I was just watching the kids play, and they were screaming out to their friends, "Hit 'em with the Shammgod! The Shammgod, the Shammgod, the Shammgod . . ."

It was surreal. It took on a life of its own. Before things were going viral, it went viral. I guess ESPN *SportsCenter* was replaying the clip the whole next day, and it made the Top 10 Plays, and people were running to their VCRs to record it and show it to all their homeboys.

Listen, I am not naive. I have to thank God for his divine timing. I did a one-handed crossover, and it was cool. But I'd done a move like that a hundred times before. I'd done even better moves at the Rucker, if I'm being honest.

But I just so happened to do it on national television back when everybody was still sitting around the TV, watching the same station. And my name just so happened to be God Shammgod and not Frank Jones or Derrick Jefferson.

If I did the same thing, at the same time, do you think kids would still be yelling out, "Yo, hit him with the Frank!"

Hell no.

I remember my guy Allen Iverson always coming up to me and shaking his head, saying, "Man, if only my momma had named me 'God.' I'd have been selling so many shoes, bro."

What can I say? I was blessed. Not just with my name. But with my whole history. With my whole DNA. With my whole *life*—all the good and all the bad.

Everything that I am went into that move.

I tried so hard for ten-plus years to do it. I tried it 17 million times. I tried it when I was hungry and cold and broke as hell. I tried it until everybody at the park was laughing at me, calling me nutso. I tried it and I failed and failed and failed. Until one day, it finally worked.

March 23, 1997.

My body went right, my soul went left.

And I finally shook my own shadow.

Everybody knows exactly where they were on the morning of March 9, 1997. You might've been out on the corner, or sitting in front of the TV eating breakfast, or waiting to catch the bus. I happened to be sitting in my dorm room at Providence. It was the week before we left for that unforgettable March Madness run. All I was thinking about was basketball. All of a sudden, somebody in the dorm came running down the halls, talking about "Biggie got shot! Yo, Biggie got shot! They're saying it was a drive-by!"

Instantly, I was scared for Mase. At that point in time, we were both off doing our thing, living two separate lives, but we'd always catch up with one another on the phone, and I knew that he was out in Los Angeles with Big for the Soul Train Awards. He could've easily been in the car with Big that night, but I found out later that he went back to the hotel instead of going to the after-party.

By the time we turned the TVs on, it was already headline news. You know it's fucked-up when you see the older white lady on CNN talking about "Christopher Wallace." Whenever you see the full name on the screen, you know somebody is already gone. Biggie was dead at twenty-four. *Biggie*. Yo—we're talking about *Biggie*. It's hard for kids growing up now to understand how monumental that moment was in black culture. In the span of six months, 2Pac and Biggie were both killed in drive-bys. Two of the greatest rappers—no, see, that's not even taking it far enough— two of the most influential figures in the history of black culture were taken from us. All the beef and everything that was going on in the streets at that time, it didn't feel real until people really started dying. Then it was *too real*. When Pac got killed, I was literally grieving for months. I never even got the chance to meet Pac, but our families' backgrounds were so similar with the Black Panthers and the Five Percenters, and as I got older everybody always used to say that I looked like him. I was raised in Bad Boy country, but Pac was my guy, and I let everybody know it. I let Big know it! When Pac died, it was like I lost a family member. And then for Big to get killed six months later, it felt like the world was falling apart. It was the same feeling as when Rich Porter got murdered, only on a national level. It felt like the end of a golden era, and the start of a darker chapter. Once that cycle of revenge starts, nowhere feels safe. I was worried for Mase.

In the hood, we have a complicated relationship with success. All you ever want to do when you're growing up in Harlem is to get up out of there and see the world. But when you actually do it, then all you want to do is come back and see your people and feel that feeling of home again. They say it's money that's the root of all evil, right? But I think you can go deeper than that. It's not just money. It's jealousy. I've seen guys get killed over $50 and $50,000. The amount doesn't make the difference. It's all about jealousy. If you got $5 more than some dudes, that's a problem for them. They want to chop you down.

When Mase first blew up and got his deal, I got to see the dangers of fame up close and personal. I'll never forget, he came to pick me up one day at my building on 142nd Street. By that time, he was staying downtown in a nice apartment. But he'd always come uptown to see his people. He parked the whip—something ridiculous, something foreign, I forget which one it was—but he parked on the corner and we went into the corner store. On my block, he didn't have to worry about a thing. Nobody was going to bother him. So he didn't have no bodyguard, no gun, nothing.

We're not thinking about anything but getting some chips or something. We come out of the store and this light-skinned dude walks up on us, talking about "Got any change for a dollar?"

I'm like, "Change for a dollar? What you talking about?"

He's like, "Four quarters. Help me out."

I'm looking in my pockets. Mase is looking at me, all confused.

It was exactly like when I got my burgers snatched when I was seven years old. This light-skinned dude *bamboozled* us. He played the Jedi mind trick on us. We were looking in our pockets like, "Nah, homie, I don't think—"

All of a sudden, before I even know what's going on, I'm staring down the barrel of a gun.

He's pointing it at me, and he's telling Mase, "Take off all the jewelry, or I'm gonna kill your friend."

Mase took a step like he was going to run, and the dude put the gun right to my head.

He said, "If you run, I'm gonna shoot him right now."

Mase took off his chain and put it on the ground. But the dude wanted his Rolex too.

He said, "Take off the watch, or I'm gonna fucking kill your boy right now."

Then he said something so crazy, that I still think about it to this day.

He said, "I might kill y'all anyway."

There's a way that people talk when they're serious and when they're bluffing. You get attuned to that in the hood. And I didn't think the dude was bluffing. Not got no mask on. This was a setup. Is this a robbery, or a murder? After all this shit, after all the blood, sweat, and tears, I'm finally about to make it out of here . . . and now I'm going to die outside the corner store? This can't be the way I'm going out . . .

Mase slowly took off the Rollie and slipped it from his wrist, and then he did something that I've only ever seen in the movies. He threw the Rollie up into the air so the dude would take his eyes off me. He lowered the gun for a second to catch the watch, and Mase yelled, "Shamm, runnnnnnn!!!"

We ran for our lives.

All you're doing at that point is listening for the shots and praying.

We ran around the corner, and as soon as we did, we saw an NYPD car chilling right there. I've never been so happy to see a cop. We ran up to the window like, "Yo! Help! Dude over there got a gun!"

Right at that moment, this light-skinned motherfucker came running around the corner and saw the cops. Like a cartoon, son. "Ruh-rohh!" They snatched up this dude like on *Scooby-Doo*. You know when they catch the evildoer at the end of the episode and they rip the mask off? They were cuffing him right in front of us, putting him in the car, and we're just standing there breathing the air like we never breathed that shit before. Just thankful to be alive.

NYPD was looking at Mase like, "You look *familiar*."

That was a hard lesson for us. I think back on that day all the time, because it was the last day that Mase and Shamm could just be Mase and Shamm. It was the last time we could just talk up to the corner store, like we were back at PS92. We had to start a new chapter. We had to grow. We had to get up out of the hood.

After that wild March Madness in '97, I had to make a decision. People were telling me that if I declared for the NBA Draft, I was going to be a late first round pick. I was going to be a millionaire, guaranteed. It was a sure thing. With one word— "Okay"—I could change my family's circumstances forever. The thing is, everything happened so fast for me that I wasn't even thinking about leaving school before that tournament. In my head, I was going to be at Providence for another two years. I was going to get my degree, and then I'd try making some real money playing ball—whether that was the NBA or overseas or with the Harlem Globetrotters or something. But then after I pulled "The Shammgod," I started speaking to agents, and they were all saying, "You're hot right now. You gotta take advantage of it. If you come back and you get hurt, who knows what could happen?"

That's how the devil works. That's how he gets you. He tries to get you into your *fears*. My whole life, I was patient. I never rushed anything. I always would just sit and talk to God, and he would tell me the right path. But for some reason, with the NBA Draft, my head was never clear. It wasn't just about me this time, you feel me? It was about my son, and my mother, and my siblings. If I don't do this, am I being selfish? If I stay at Providence, I'm sleeping good. I'm in the dorms with my nice mattress pad and my meal plan. I'm eating three square meals, guaranteed. I got pocket money. But is my mother sleeping good? Is my son? Are my siblings worried about what they're gonna eat tomorrow? Everything was weighing on me. For once in my life, I wasn't seeing the bigger picture. If I had come back to school, I would've been the hottest guard in the country. I would've been on the cover of every magazine. I could've established myself as a Top 5 pick. Instead I said the word that put my life on a much different path: "Okay."

I listened to the fear, for once in my life.

I took the easy money.

I declared for the draft as a raw prospect and not a finished product.

It was the best-worst-best thing that ever happened to me. It's not even "complicated." It just *is*. When you see the bigger picture, you don't see anything as a single entity. You see every-thing as a full circle. You see everything flowing together, as God intended.

"Shamm, I thought you said you didn't drink? You trippin'?"

Listen, if you think that's too deep, then you haven't lived a real life yet. Take a word of advice from a man who stared down the barrel of a gun four or five times in his life: Things don't happen *to* you. They happen *for* you. If you live long enough, and you take a minute to reflect back on your life, you're going to see exactly what I'm talking about. The things you see as random aren't random. The things you see as mistakes aren't mistakes. They're lessons. That's just God talking to you. He's been talking to you your whole life. You just got your headphones on. You're thinking about cars, houses, shoes. It's all *noise*. You aren't listen-ing. Go sit on a bench in Harlem and look up at the sky, son. You'll hear him.

On draft night, I went to be with my people. I didn't want to be in the club. I didn't want forty-seven cameras on me, like these kids got now. (Yo, you really let your moms get you the big balloons with your jersey number? We at a third-grade birthday party? Come on son, *Soft*.) Instead, my whole family went to Aunt Viv's house. We were eating good. We were sitting around the living room, waiting. Two hours before the draft started, the New York Knicks called me. That week, everybody thought I was going to the Knicks. I worked out for them, and they loved me. They needed a point guard. God Shammgod, the Harlem kid coming home to play at the Garden. It was perfect. It was *too* perfect.

Somebody from their front office called the house, and I could tell from the dude's voice that something was off. He said, "Man, you know . . . everything should work out."

I'm thinking: *Everything should work out? Nah. I know fake when I hear fake. Your whole energy is different now. It's over.*

I hung up the phone and I hugged my son and I just started crying.

Aunt Viv was like, "What's going on? What's wrong with you?"

I said, "The Knicks aren't taking me. I can feel it."

They all thought I was tripping. But I wasn't tripping. My instincts are never wrong when it comes to people's vibes. The draft comes on the TV, and the Knicks were the 25th pick. It's not like now, where you have guys breaking the news ten minutes before the pick. Back in the day, you were watching it all unfold live just like anybody else. So the big homie David Stern comes up to the podium to announce the Knicks' pick, and the only thing that hasn't changed in all these years is that the Knicks fans were booing the commish.

Was I tripping?

Of course not.

He didn't say my name.

The Knicks took John Thomas.

Now, John Thomas is a good dude. That's my boy. But the pick didn't make any sense. They already had Charles Oakley at power forward. Charles *Oakley*, bro. They had John Wallace as the backup. This was a team that was last in assists and first in turnovers. They needed a point guard. They could've had one from right in their own backyard, who grew up scraping his knees in the public parks and dribbling through the 1 train. So yes, I felt some type of way about it. I didn't get it, even from a basketball perspective. It was a long wait the rest of that night. There's only 57 picks total. But that doesn't even do the math justice. Because there's only *so many teams* that need a point guard. I was looking at the board, I knew I was *really* down to two to three teams. At that point, you're just praying to hear your name. You never thought it could feel so good for an old white man in a suit to call you to the front of the class.

Finally, at pick 45, I heard my name.

The Washington Wizards selected "God Shammgod, point guard, Providence College."

Just like that, I had made it to the NBA.

All my bitterness washed away. All my anxiety. All my fears. I would have played anywhere. I would have played on the moon. It was the happiest moment of my life, after the birth of my son. I remember hugging my mother, and she was crying, and I will always remember the way that hug felt. She was saying, "Wow. You really did it. I'm so proud of you."

From when I was super young, I always wanted to be the man that she never had for herself. I wanted to be a rock for her. I wanted to be somebody that she could always count on. I wanted to fill that void. That night, when I got picked, I finally felt like I could exhale. When they said my name, it felt like I had saved *both* of our lives. The sword isn't hanging over our heads anymore. The fridge is always gonna be full. The electric bill is staying paid. My brother and sister can go back-to-school shopping and fill up the cart. We don't have to worry about basic things ever again. That's what it means to *really* make it. Not the cars and the jewelry. All that can be leased. All that can be snatched right off your neck. All that is just for flexing. It's hollow. Nah, really making it in the hood is knowing that the fridge is full, *forever*.

But money is funny. It's all a matter of perspective. When you're young, you don't understand the difference between rich and *rich rich*. I got schooled on that quick, as soon as I got down to DC and I started hanging out with Rod Strickland, Chris Webber, and Juwan Howard. What? You're surprised? You thought that God was just going to put random teammates around me? Come on, son. We're eleven chapters into this thing. You know I only hang around *legends*.

Rod was a New York City kid, and I knew C-Webb and Juwan from playing in tournaments growing up. They weren't just teammates, they were the *homies*. I'll never forget, I got humbled so quick . . . I was in the locker room during one of the first weeks of training camp, and my locker was three stalls down from Juwan. In the NBA they don't give you your salary in a lump sum. We got paid every two weeks, like a regular corporate job. Back in the day, before direct deposit, somebody would show up from the accounting department and literally hand out the checks. My first season, I wasn't even making a million a year. With endorsements and everything, I was probably clearing a mil. But my actual salary as a second rounder was like $800,000. So I'm young and naive, right? I don't know *nothing* about federal, state, and local. Social Security. Medicare. Union dues? What union? The Soviet Union? I'm twenty. I got a lawyer who thinks about all that stuff. Just give me that check, and whatever's on the total is gonna be more money than I've ever seen in my life.

So the bagman comes in and hands out everybody's checks after practice, and I'm looking at mine, holding it up to the light and everything, just looking at all the zeroes. *Damn.*

Twenty-five thousand dollars. For *me*. Pay to the order of: GOD SHAMMGOD. Twenty-five *thou*. And *another* twenty-five thou coming in two weeks? For real? I felt like the richest man in the world. I felt like I was *getting away with something*. How can they let us do this? We're playing ball for 25K every two weeks? It's preposterous. I'd play for free.

I'm smiling ear to ear.

A couple weeks go by, and we get another round of checks, and of course, I *need* mine, because I've been to the mall and back about sixteen times. The bagman hands Juwan his check, and everybody in the locker room is laughing. They're telling Juwan, "Yo, let me see that. Let me just hold it, dog. I bet that thing is *heavy*."

I didn't understand what was going on. I walk over to Juwan, and he's holding up the check to everybody. And I'm looking at the numbers and I see . . .

Yo. *What?*

I feel like I'm hallucinating. I'm seeing more zeroes than I've ever seen in my life. I'm seeing multiple commas. They can barely fit the fucking zeroes in the little box where you supposed to write the number. They had to color outside the lines, there was so many zeroes.

Juwan's check says $6 million.

Six million dollars and zero cents.

I felt dyslexic.

I said, "That say six hundred thousand?"

Juwan said, "Nah, you're missing a zero, Shamm. Six mil."

Welcome to the NBA, rookie. I almost fainted.

I'm like, "My check is twenty-five thousand dollars! How are you getting the big Publishers Clearinghouse check, son? Yo, I gotta fire my agent!"

Everybody was cracking up. I didn't realize that when you sign the Big Dog deals, they have to give you a certain percentage up front.

I'm telling Juwan and C-Webb, "Yo, I'm *broke*. You need to buy me dinner tonight. I'm about to get on welfare again, son."

C-Webb would be pulling up to practice with TVs in his car that were bigger than the TV in my *apartment*. That's the first time I ever heard somebody talking about "my chef."

I'm like, "Yo, you so rich you opened up a *restaurant* in your own house? *Damn*. I thought I had money because I wasn't looking at the Dollar Menu no more."

That's when I realized that there was levels to this game.

C-Webb is probably going to kill me for telling this story, but I have to keep it real for the people. The thing about C-Webb is that the ladies *loved* this man. Listen, just to be clear, C-Webb is a family man now. We've all settled down. But I knew him when we were still kids, and the ladies used to flock to this man like nothing I've ever seen in my *life*. You remember how Jason Terry's father used to talk about me at Providence? That's how I am when I talk about C-Webb and women.

"C-Webb, I never seen anything like you in my liiiiife!"

He always used to tell me, "Listen, Shamm, I know those rookie checks burn up fast when you got your people relying on you, so if you ever need me to spot you some money, just come and see me and I'll take care of you."

On one of our first road trips, I needed some money for the weekend, so I asked CB in the locker room if he could spot me two hundred dollars.

He said, "Yeah, no problem. Come to my hotel room when we get back."

Mannnn. I come knocking on this man's hotel room later that night, and he's already got the do-not-disturb sign on the knob. I knock anyway. Silence. I'm waiting . . . I'm waiting. The door opens just a crack. I hear this nice female voice, whispering.

"Yes?"

"It's Shammgod. Is C-Webb here?"

"Chris is laying down right now."

"Can you just tell him I'm here?"

"Hold on one moment."

Door closes.

I'm waiting there, thinking: *This man is a legend. How does he do it? Even the voice was fly.*

Two minutes go by, and the door opens up again, this time about halfway. The hand comes out first. It's holding a fat stack of twenties.

Then I see the nicest smile I've ever seen.

She says, "Chris said to give you this. And to have a nice time."

It was Tyra Banks, standing there in a T-shirt.

Tyra Banks handed me five hundred dollars and told me to have a nice time.

She closed the door and I was just standing there holding the wall, trying to catch my breath, like: "Yo . . . was that . . . Nah. Wait. *What?*"

You ever see that meme of the dude from *The Wire* with his hand on his chin, looking around like he got his mind blown? That was me.

I walked into practice the next day and C-Webb is looking at me like nothing happened. Like it was just another day. I said, "Bro, was that who I think it was? From the tee-vee?"

He's just staring at me like it's Tuesday. He shrugs his shoulders. "Yeah."

I said, "Man, what do I have to do to get a girl like that? What do my checks gotta be? Teach me, C-Webb."

He said, "First thing you need to do is, you need to calm down, son."

Welcome to the NBA, rook.

On the court, it was the same thing. I was having a hard time adjusting to a whole new world. "The Shammgod" was the ultimate blessing and the ultimate curse when it came to my NBA career. Everywhere I went, that's all anybody wanted to see. I started feeling like I was a sideshow, and not a real NBA player. It's so funny, because people always associate me with "And 1," because the street basketball stuff became huge in the early 2000s, but I literally never had anything to do with And 1. That came *after* my time. When I was a rookie in the league, I was like an anomaly. Nobody was dribbling like I was dribbling. AI was doing his thing, but he was a different player than I was. He was more of a complete scorer. "The Shammgod" blowing up like it did kind of sparked this whole subculture around creativity and dribbling, but the coaches didn't want to see it.

I'm always joking with these young NBA dudes now, "Man, my moms had me twenty years too early. If I popped out when you did, I'd be worth four hundred million dollars and some change. These old coaches were looking at me like I *snuck in the building* through the back door."

This was the golden era of the Big Man. You had Shaquille O'Neal, Hakeem Olajuwon, David Robinson, Patrick Ewing, Alonzo Mourning, Dikembe Mutombo . . . The NBA was more of a system league. And if you were a point guard, the coaches didn't want you "overdribbling." They just wanted you to get the ball to the big fella as quickly as possible. And it's so funny because the coaches wanted one thing from me, and the fans and even the other players wanted the exact opposite.

I'll never forget playing against Gary Payton for the first time. GP is obviously the undisputed heavyweight champion of shit-talking. But I mean, I'm from *Harlem*. You can't say nothing to me I haven't heard before. We in the NBA, right? Nobody got a tool over in the backpack on the sideline. So I'm chilling. What's he going to say to me?

Mannnnn. We get out onto the court, and he never shut up. He was relentless. And this is a *preseason* game, mind you. The crowd is half-full. You could hear a pin drop in there, and GP is doing his GP voice: "Ey. Ey. Ey. Young fella. You think you the God of dribbling? You think you special? Ey. Ey. Young fella. I'm talking to you."

GP is the heavyweight champion because he never stops. He never catches his breath. He gives you no choice but to respond.

"Come on, man. Let's play ball."

"Oh, you wanna play ball? You think you can cross me up? You need *Jesus*. You ain't *shit*."

That's when I realized that I kind of had a target on my back. Right away, basketball felt a little bit different to me. My entire life, it was my release. Whenever I had a basketball in my hand, it was the exact same feeling, whether I was all alone in the park, or I was playing at the Rucker, or I was playing in the Big East. All I ever felt was joy. I never had a father who was pushing me to be the next Jordan. I never had a mother who was telling me that I had to make it so I could buy her a house. It was all me. I was doing it purely for the love of it. But when I got to the NBA, basketball started to feel like a business.

By the end of my rookie year, I was struggling to get minutes. I felt like in every arena I walked into, all anybody wanted to do was see The Shammgod. But if you've been paying attention to this story, then you already know that it's not something that you can just do on command. This ain't *2K*, young boy. You don't hit R2 and Circle and the move just triggers. It has to be natural. You have to be in the flow of the game, and then it just spontaneously comes out of you. I felt like I was being boxed in. I'd have 10 assists in a game, and fans would literally be screaming "Do the move!" I'd have other players coming up to me in warm-ups, like, "Yo, Shamm. Can you show me how to do that move?"

Man, *Shaq* came up to me when we were playing the Lakers. During the shootaround. He comes walking up with a big smile on his face. Walking like Shaq, talking like Shaq. I mean, it's *Shaq*. I was watching this dude in *Blue Chips*, and now he's real.

"Young fella. Can you teach me that move?"

I'm like, "Uhhh . . . Big fella, I don't know about that. I can try."

What was I gonna say? It's Shaq.

I'm like, "Alright, it's all in the feet. That's what people don't understand."

I'm doing a dribbling tutorial in the middle of the Staples Center. It was crazy. Kobe is looking over just shaking his damn head, like: *Man, I remember this shit.*

I remember after that game, Kobe invited me to come over to his crib, and he lived way up in the hills. I didn't know anything about Los Angeles. I had only ever seen it in the movies. My reference was *Boyz n the Hood—imdb*. All that street-level South Central stuff. So I didn't even know you could live way up in the hills like that. Kobe had the craziest house I'd ever seen up to that point. He had the waterfall pool before that was even a thing. I remember walking around the place and telling him, "You're living like Eddie Murphy in *Boomerang*, son."

The funny part was, they weren't even playing Kobe that many minutes yet. He was still misunderstood at that time, coming into the league from high school. They were calling him a showboat. They were calling me a street act. We were both going through it. We sat around his kitchen and ended up talking for hours, and I remember telling him, "Yo, you're gonna be alright." And he was telling me the same. I'll never forget walking to the edge of his property and looking out over the whole city of Los Angeles, and all the yellow and orange lights were twinkling just like you see in the movies, and it was like the soundtrack started playing in my head, you know what I'm saying? That Dolby surround sound logo. I was seeing the MGM lion. The credits started up. Only we were really living it. I got goose bumps. I turned to Kobe and said, "Man, remember when we were back in the gym at ABCD camp? I didn't think you was gonna be *shit*. We came a long way, France."

At the end of the day, my NBA career didn't turn out how I wanted it to. I was never getting those $6 million checks like my boy Juwan. But I got memories that are worth $60 million. I got memories that nobody can ever take away from me. We grew up thinking that Madison Square Garden was off-limits to us. We thought that it existed in another physical realm, where they didn't let in kids like us. We stood outside places like that a hundred times and just looked at the facade, but we never thought we'd ever get inside, unless somebody's cousin hooked us up with a job selling popcorn. The first time I ever ran out of the tunnel at MSG as an NBA player, with my whole family watching, with the name SHAMMGOD on the back of my jersey, that is a moment that nobody can ever take away from me. To me, it was bigger than being an All-Star. It was bigger than being in the Hall of Fame. I *was* that dude on the grainy VHS tape we used to watch, you feel me? I was in the building. I was on the floor. I was a miracle.

I'll never forget playing against the Bulls for the first time in Chicago, and I was doing my thing a couple hours before shoot-around. They always made the rookies go out and work out two hours before the game. It was just me and a few guys. No music. No fans. Nothing. And then I looked over to the other side of the court, and the first thing I saw was the Jordans. It was really *those* Js. And then I saw the socks. It was really *those* socks. And then I saw the shorts. It was really *those* shorts. And then I saw the bald head. And it was really Jordan. It was MJ live and in the flesh. Shooting just like MJ shoot. Walking just like MJ walk. Talking just like MJ talk.

Hold up, is he talking to *me?*

"Shammgod!"

He's talking to me. MJ knows my name.

"Hey, Shammgod!"

I said, "Mike?"

I'm looking behind me like: *You talking to me?*

He said, "Man, you owe me *money.*"

"What?"

"Why'd you let that motherfucker shoot the shot at the end of the game!"

"What?"

"Man, I *bet* on y'all against Arizona."

"Oh, damn. I'm sorry, Mike. I'm sorry, dog!"

Hahhahahahaha. Yo! *Is he serious?*

I said, "Man, I'm just happy you know my name. I just want to thank you for everything you've done for the NBA. I grew up watching you."

He said, "Cool. You still owe me money."

How much is that memory worth? Sixty million? Nah, it's priceless.

But I think the craziest moment was the first time we played in Minnesota against Steph and KG. I'm coming out for warm-ups in front of all these people and all these cameras, and all I can think about when I see Steph is how we used to be standing in front of the mirror, trying to give fake postgame interviews like Kenny Anderson. Now kids in the stands got on Marbury jerseys. Surreal, son. But that wasn't the best part. The best part was what they were blasting on the speakers in the arena.

I'm on the sideline stretching and Steph comes up running over to me wide-eyed, pointing up at the jumbotron.

He said, "Yooooo! *Tell* me that's the same kid you brung around to Coney Island back in the day!!! That *can't* be the same kid, B!"

I said, "The very same."

"Nah. For real?"

"Murder Mase on the mic."

"NAHHHH!"

Mase had just dropped *Harlem World* a few months before that, and the single was blowing up. They were playing it during warm-ups in every NBA arena that year.

Steph is cracking up, singing:

Bad bad bad bad boy
You make me feel so good!

He said, "Man, I remember dude rappin' for Chinese food on the corner in Coney Island. Now he's in the music video with *Chris Tucker*? I thought I was tripping when I seen that. That's *crazy*."

I said, "Yo, we all came a long, long, *long* way, huh?"

How much is that moment worth? Six hundred million? Nah. Three grubby New York City kids on top of the world? That's *priceless*.

That same year, I finally got into the Apollo Theater. All my *life*, I walked by that red neon sign. I used to sit in KC's clothing store as a kid and just stare at that WELCOME TO THE WORLD FAMOUS APOLLO marquee. But I had never been up in that joint. As a matter of fact, I'd never even been to a concert before. But then Mase blew up, and he was playing the Apollo one night, and he got me backstage. I remember walking in there and just being in awe of the place. The red seats. The opera boxes. The velvet curtains. It was everything we saw on TV. It was really there in our neighborhood that whole time, you know what I mean? It was like I stepped into another world. I'll never forget standing on the side of the stage when Mase walked out, and everybody was going crazy. My guy had the biggest smile on his face. He starts rapping, like I've seen him rap ten million times before. And I knew he was doing what he loved to do. I started thinking about how he used to be rapping at house parties, and the shorties used to be getting *so* annoyed. "Nobody wants to hear that! We're trying to listen to Boyz II Men, *dummy!*"

I started thinking about how he used to be doing the "crab dribble" in the middle of the cafeteria at PS92, and all the kids would be banging on the tables, driving the teachers crazy.

I started thinking about how I'd drag this dude to the park with me every morning before school to play *defense* for me, just so I could work on my handle, and how he never complained.

I started thinking about the fight we had in the park before I left for Providence, talking shit, going for each other's *souls*, like:

"Man, you think you gonna be Biggie? You ain't never gonna be no rapper."

"Yeah? You think you gonna be Isiah? Come on, son. You ain't never gonna play in the NBA. Be real."

"Okay, Big."

"Okay, Isiah."

"Alright, you wanna get some Chinese?"

"Beef 'n' broccoli do sound good. You got any money?"

"Nah, you?"

"*Nah.* We'll figure it out . . ."

The earth spins twice. It all comes around again. Everything you are now, it has roots in the past. If you don't believe that, then you haven't lived a real life. Listen to me: *the earth spins twice.*

Mase was always a performer. Ever since he was ten years old. Now he was just doing it at the World Famous Apollo. The same Mason Betha. The same big smile. The same big heart.

Watching him up there doing this thing, I started sobbing. I was crying tears of joy.

I will take that memory with me to my grave. I wasn't just looking at my first friend in the world. It was deeper than that. I was looking at the American Dream.

12

Real talk: I think I spent most of my life functionally depressed.

I never realized this until I was about forty-four years old, and I went back to Harlem to visit one of my boys. He was living in the same project building we grew up in. It wasn't even that late at night. It was like eleven o' clock. But when I got out of the car, nobody was around, and it was dark, and I walked into that building, and I smelled that *smell*. It's the smell that always brings me back in time. The light was flickering, like it always flickers in the projects. I hit the elevator button, and it took forever, like it always takes in the projects. There was piss on the floor. I remember looking down at my shoes, and stepping around the puddle, and I had the strangest sensation come over me, waiting for the elevator doors to open. I was *nervous*. I was a grown man, and I was actually nervous.

I grew up in the same building at eleven, twelve, thirteen years old, living around stick-up crews and killers every single day, walking back from the park at two o' clock in the morning, waiting for this same elevator, and I was never scared.

How is that possible? How the fuck did I make it out of here? I was literally transported back in time waiting for that elevator to come, and I was scared for my younger self.

I stepped inside the elevator and I hit the button, and I tucked my necklace inside my shirt instinctively, and I was counting the seconds till those elevator doors closed and I was safe.

One . . . two . . . three . . . four . . . five . . .

Damn, Shamm. How did you survive? How did you live like this every day?

There's only one way I can explain it.

A fish who was born in water don't know what *water* is, you feel me?

When you grow up in the environment that I grew up in, you deal with so much trauma that you just *normalize* the trauma. You're so used to bad things happening all around you that whenever somebody gets killed, you learn to just say, "Damn, that's crazy," and you keep it moving.

It's incredible the things that your mind can just block out. My freshman year of college, I got a phone call from back home. One of *them* calls. Out of the blue.

"Yo, they found your stepfather."

"What you mean found him?"

"I don't know, bro. They found him layin' on the sidewalk."

"He drunk?"

"Nah, bro. He's gone."

"What?"

"They think he fell off the fire escape or something."

That was it. I don't remember no police report. I don't remember no funeral. If I was there, I blocked it out. I never asked any follow-up questions. I just played a movie of it in my mind, to try to explain it. In Harlem, we used to go up on the fire escapes all the time. Drinking, smoking, or just a moment of peace. That's the Harlem front porch, man. Sometimes you'd climb up the ladder and go through the kitchen window if you were locked out. I'd done it a thousand times. That's just New York City. Did he slip? Was he drunk? Was he just tired as a dog from working all the time, and he lost his grip? Did somebody push him? Did he jump?

To this day, I don't have answers.

I just kept it moving.

I don't even think I ever talked with my mother about it ever again. Ain't that crazy?

What am I gonna do? Grieve? Ain't got time to grieve. I got practice tomorrow. I gotta make All–Big East. I gotta make the tournament. I gotta get in front of these NBA scouts. I gotta, I gotta, I gotta . . .

In the hood, you never really process anything. You don't got time. So you learn to be numb to everything. You keep looking straight ahead. It's fucked-up, but it's the truth. Even when I almost got shot when I was fifteen, running down that alley, you know what all the bystanders were doing when that car sped off, and it was all over?

They were laughing.

I'll never forget that.

I was walking back down the block in shock, and an older dude was sitting on the stoop. He saw it all go down, and he was cracking up, like, "Son, why would you think you could outrun a *car*?"

They say you got two choices when you grow up in that environment. You can either laugh or you can cry. I chose the third option. I was just *blank*. I carried that attitude with me into my adult life.

When my NBA dream ended, I didn't react at all.

I never got fired from a job in my life, because the only two jobs I ever had was sweeping the floors at the West Indian joint and playing in the NBA. I got injured midway through the season, and I could tell that I was in trouble. I thought they were going to trade me. But when the trade deadline came and went and I was still on the team, my coach Bernie Bickerstaff called me into his office.

Bernie said, "I don't think we're going to be able to keep you."

I said, "What does that mean?"

He said, "It means we're going to release you."

I said, "Okay. Thank you."

I got up and walked out of the room, and I started my new life. No emotion. Nothing. I thought that was just how I remembered it in my head, but years later, I was catching up with Bernie, and he confirmed it was just like that. He said, "Man, that was the weirdest player exit I've ever had in my whole career. You just stood up, said thank you, and walked out of the building."

In the hood, you don't have any time to ask yourself *Why*. You just have to move forward and figure it out. Because if you don't

Mom from back in the '70s.

I told you that my father was a boss. Just look at him.

My beautiful mom, always with a smile on her face.

God Shammgod and Baby God Shammgod.

Little Shamm, probably looking for some food or a toy to throw around.

Only in my story could my Harlem PE teacher turn out to be NBA legend Nate "Tiny" Archibald.

In Harlem with Moms and my sister.

Yep, that's really who you think it is on the right. My boy Meta World Peace aka Ron Artest.

McDonald's All-American game, chilling with Chauncey Billups, Vince Carter, Antawn Jamison, and Kevin Garnett.

Me with coach and Marbury.

Crossing 'em up at the McDonald's All-American Game.

My first-born came out the womb looking fly, like every kid in Harlem.

Me and Stephon Marbury back in the day. Yo, I need to find that leather jacket.

Me, Steph, and Biggie Smalls kicking it at the Tunnel nightclub.

Reunited with my old friend "France."

Only took me twenty years, but I graduated from Providence with a fire GPA.

Me and my man Nipsey Hussle—rest in peace, legend.

Me with the best pure shooter to ever do it, Steph Curry.

Me and Kyrie.

Release of my first shoe with Puma.
I used to dream of days like this.

Teaching my son how to get in a proper
New York City subway nap.

My son Amir said, "Dad, why'd you beat New York?"

My son Eryk. The Garden loves Daddy. When dreams come true.

With my son Prince. The love of the game!

Me and Jay-Z, cracking up together since the late '80s.

Just getting a little better every day, with Harrison Barnes.

With me and Luka Dončić, it's always been love since day one.

Telling a story to LL Cool J courtside.

Yes, I even taught Dirk Nowitzki how to do "The Shammgod."

Damian Lillard is and will always be a REAL ONE.

Who would have thought the kid from Harlem would have his own signature Puma shoe?

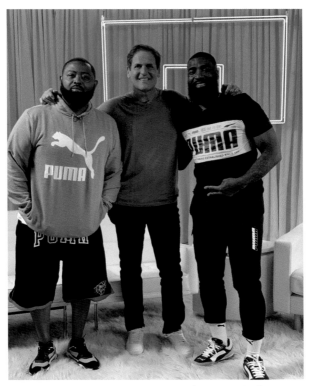

If there's one guy I owe my second act to, it's the one and only Mark Cuban.

Me, Allen Iverson, and Steve Francis, talking shit to one another like we've been doing for thirty years!

Me and Cam'ron. *Cam, why you looking so serious?* You got too much money to be frowning.

Asking Ice Cube when the next Friday movie is coming out.

Connecting with a fellow Point God, Chris Paul.

Has there ever been anybody scarier going to the hoop than my boy Russell Westbrook?

As a teacher, my job is not to be your "yes-man." It's to punish you. Band work!

My son God Shammgod Jr. following in his pops' footsteps.

figure it out, you're going to be dead or out on the streets. After only one season in the NBA—just twenty games total because of injuries—my career in the league was over. I was doing some workouts for teams that offseason, but nobody was interested. At that point in time, nobody had seen people in the league like me and Iverson and Steph. The culture was starting to shift, but people weren't ready for us. And listen, I get it. I'm coming into practice with durags on. I got guys in different cities coming to say what's up to me at the hotel, and they got Rollies on, and they definitely are not lawyers, you feel me? They're not in private equity. Well, they are. They're in a different kind of private equity. I had assistant coaches looking at me like I was Don Corleone. They didn't even try to understand.

I tell my players now, when they're coming into the arena rocking the durag with the headphones on and the Malcolm X T-shirt: "Man, y'all boys don't know how I *suffered* for you to be able to do this shit. You walking straight past the media with the Beats on, dog? I didn't even have a Walkman. I was just trying to get a little wavey and these people were calling me a thug. Y'all *owe me money*."

They don't know how it was! I'm not trying to make anybody feel sorry for me, because they were crucifying AI at that time, too. But AI was a finished product. You couldn't argue with his game. I was still raw. When I tried out for teams, they didn't see the potential. They just saw the headlines. I honestly think they just saw a headache. And I think that's what hurt me the most— that people questioned how seriously I took the game. If you've been paying attention to anything in this book, then you know that I gave my entire life to basketball. I would've played it for a bag of chips. But when I got to the league, it just didn't feel the same. It was like everybody was looking at me as an action figure instead of a basketball player. All anybody wanted to see was my crossover. It got to the point when the crowd would be yelling my name, and it was filling me with anxiety. Because I didn't know if they were screaming "Shammgod! Shammgod!" for me or for the move. My legs started feeling heavy. My head started feeling heavy. At first I was mad that I wasn't playing. But then I didn't even care. That's when you know you got a real problem. If a basketball player is pissed-off that he's on the bench, that's good. That's healthy. If he don't care, then he's depressed.

For me, at the end of my rookie year, basketball just didn't feel fun anymore. And I really fell out of love with the game for a minute. The functional depression became not so functional. For the first time in my life, I wasn't popping out of bed with a smile on my face and grabbing the first basketball I saw. I was really struggling. Because now I got a whole family to provide for, and I got half of Harlem on my back, and I got my own bills to pay plus a hundred others, and the NBA checks have stopped coming.

I didn't have time to feel fear. I had to keep it moving. So I did the first thing I could think of. I went to the streets. I took $10,000 cash out of the bank and I went to see two of my boys up in Harlem. I said, "I don't want to touch anything. I don't want anybody talking to me. I'm the finance. Take the money and put it in the streets, and I'll be back in two weeks."

That's just how it is in the hood. Even the sensible ones, we all got our fallback.

I thought I was so slick. I'm like: Yo, the NBA don't want me? Alright, I'm gonna be the next KC. Nobody is even gonna know what I'm up to. I'm gonna keep my nose clean. I'm gonna be sponsoring AAU teams. I'm gonna have my little empire. I'm gonna be building schools, son. I'm gonna do it the way nobody thought to do it before . . .

Mannnnnn.

I came back two weeks later, and these two silly motherfuckers are out on the corner with new winter coats on. North Face with the puffy hoods.

I'm looking all fake-tough. Stomping up to them. I'm imitating the movies.

I said, "Where's my money?"

They said, "We had some business expenses. It was cold."

"Yo, where's my *money*?"

"Come back next month. You'll get it. Chill."

"That's my last *ten thou*, son!"

"Yo, don't you play in the *NBA*?"

"Yeah. No. Maybe. *Shit*. I dunno."

They were cracking up. I was literally flabbergasted. That's the only word for it. I'm standing on the corner just shaking my head, looking up to the skies. What am I gonna do? Kill these dudes?

I knew right then and there that I was never gonna see that money again. And I knew without a shadow of a doubt that I didn't have it in me to be no *kingpin*. I don't know what I was thinking. I was just looking for any path forward.

I said, "Yo, whatever. Keep warm, B. Peace."

And I left. I was trying to keep moving forward like I'd done my whole life, but for the first time, there was nowhere left to go. I hit the end of the road. I was staring down into the abyss. That period felt biblical. It wasn't just the end of an era. It was the end of a millennium. The '90s were ending. The year 2000 was coming. Harlem was a dangerous place. In February, in the middle of winter, Big L was standing out on the corner—on *his* corner—the rapper's corner on 139th Street, when a car pulled up on him.

They shot him nine times. Big L was murdered on his *own corner*. The guy I used to argue about basketball with, the guy I used to argue about Biggie and Jay-Z with, the guy who was the inspiration for everybody I knew in our hood to start rhyming . . . He got killed on his own corner, over a neighborhood beef.

Darkness, B.

Darkness.

First Pac.

Then Biggie.

Now Big L.

Plus a hundred other brothers you never ever heard of. Gone too soon. Over *what*?

Harlem was not a safe place. New York was not a safe place. *America* was not a safe place. Ever since I was a little kid, from the moment I got my burgers snatched out of my damn hands by a grown man, I was never really fazed by anything. I buried everything inside and just kept it moving. I repeated something over and over to myself, like my own little mantra.

"It's gonna be aight, it's gonna be aight, it's gonna be aight . . ."

In the winter of 1999, for the first time in my life, a sneaky thought came into my head, and I couldn't get rid of it.

Damn . . . Maybe we're not gonna be aight.

A couple months later, Mase shocked the world. He randomly called into Hot 97 while Funkmaster Flex was live on the air, and he announced that he was retiring from the rap game. They thought he was joking. They thought it had to be a publicity stunt. But he was dead serious. Three years after he blew up and went quadruple-platinum and was on the cover of every magazine, he was done. Nothing like it had ever happened before. People were stunned. But me, I wasn't stunned at all. You never know what people are actually going through in their real lives. From the outside, all you see is the car they're driving or the jewelry they got on, but you have no idea the things they're dealing with. You don't know the pressure they might be under or what actually makes them tick. In the material realm, Mase had everything you could ever want. But he was searching for something deeper.

When he was at his lowest moment, my boy found God, and he decided to go on a different path in life. He traded in his chains and his cars and he became a pastor down in Atlanta. For some reason, me and Mase have always been linked. We both lived out our wildest dreams at the same time, and then in the snap of a finger, it was over.

What next? What was this all for? What was my purpose?

I did a lot of praying at that time. But the thing is, I wasn't asking God *for* things. I was just asking him to *use* me for something.

A couple weeks later, I got a lifeline. A scout from China had seen me working out for some teams, and they invited me over to play in some exhibition games. My agent called me and told me about it, and the first thing I said was, "China? *Hell no* I'm not going to go to no China."

Then he said, "They'll pay you fifty thousand for one month."

And I said, "What time does the flight leave?"

I didn't even know where I was going. Beijing? I know Beijing. Shanghai? I heard of that. My agent said, "No, you're going to . . . hang on . . . let me find it . . . You're going to a place called Zhe . . . Zhejiang."

"Spell it for me."

"Z . . ."

"They even got basketball over there?"

"Oh yeah, they got basketball. They love it."

"They got a *team?* What's the name?"

"The uh . . . Zhejiang Squirrels."

"The Squirrels? For real?"

"Think of the marketing potential. Big."

"Yo, is this legit? Am I about to be kidnapped? I seen movies that start this way. I'm gonna get *tooken.*"

"It says here the Zhejiang Squirrels of the China Basketball Association. It seems very legit."

"Fifty thou?"

"Fifty thou."

"For one month?"

"One month."

"Book the damn flight."

"Booking the damn flight!"

Click.

This was the year 2000, mind you. No Google Maps, dog. No iPhone. You wanna get on the internet back then, it's sounding like you're working at NASA. You're dialing into the mainframe. You remember that dial-up sound? With the static and the alarms going off? We're in a whole different era. So I'm looking for Zhejiang to figure out where I'm going, and I'm looking at a *map* map. The kind you roll up and *unfurl* and shit.

"Alright. China. Other side of the world. Cool. Found it. Where the hell is this Zhejiang . . . ?"

After about ten minutes, I found it on the map. It was a real place. And apparently the money was real. That's all I cared about. So I got on a plane, and I went to China. I land at the airport, and I'm instantly in a whole other world. This was Y2K China. We're not going to no Starbucks for a chicken salad in the plastic box. I don't see a McDonald's golden arch in sight, and *trust me*, I was looking. No, I'm in the kung fu movie, for real. I'm seeing those dope red paper lanterns outside every shop, and the yellow neon signs on the side of the buildings, and the homies carrying loads of stuff with the bamboo stick behind their heads. I've seen this movie a hundred times! Now I'm in it! Where's the temple with one thousand steps? I'm ready to learn from the ninety-nine-year-old master. Teach me how to phase through the wall, dog. I'm ready to shoot fireballs. I'm hype.

Instead, they took me to a limo. Alright, that's cool too.

The team hooked me up with this translator named Charles, and this dude knew English so good that he didn't even speak English, he spoke *American*. Charles was my boy. We were attached at the hip. I was like a little kid on a field trip. I was telling him, "Charles, don't *lose me*, son."

The second thing I noticed about China after the neon was just the sheer amount of people. I'm a city kid, but my mind was blown by how many people were walking on the streets. And 99 percent of these people had never seen a black man in their lives. Much less a black man wearing Tims and a $300 Tommy Hilfiger sweater. I'm walking through the streets with Charles and the *seas* are parting, fam. Thousands of people are looking at me like a curiosity or something. They don't know what to do. They're in awe. I'm just hearing Mandarin and it's all a blur to me. But then I *swear* I kept hearing, "Jackson, Jackson, Jackson."

Charles starts laughing.

He's like, "They're wondering if you're Michael Jackson. Or Michael Jordan. I think they're confused. That's the two black guys they know in China."

People were reaching out trying to touch my skin. Not in a malicious way. They were just amazed. They wanted to rub my arm.

I said, "Yo, tell them I'm Jordan, Jackson, Tyson, I don't care. Just tell them to chill."

It was wild. I thought these people were about to start bowing down in unison.

We get to my hotel, and it's five-star. Incredible. Bed is cozy. Shower is hot. I'm thinking: *Okay, I could get used to this.*

Charles is like, "The team would like to take you to a nice dinner tonight. Typical Chinese."

I'm like, "Chinese, huh? Cool, cool. I love Chinese. I grew up eating it every day in the hood."

Charles is laughing his ass off. He's like, "Yeah, *right.*"

We get to this Chinese spot, and I'm starving at this point. I can't wait to eat some fried rice and some beef and broccoli. Give me one hundred egg rolls with the duck sauce son.

Mannnnnn.

We walk into this place and they got a whole *aquarium* on the back wall, and Charles is pointing at it like, "Menu."

I said, "Menu?"

I don't even know what I'm looking at. I'm looking at the Pacific Ocean. I think I'm seeing tiger sharks up in there. They got Nemo swimming around, smiling at me. They got the funny homie from *The Little Mermaid*. The Lobster. He's winking at me. *Under da sea . . .*

Charles said, "Very fresh."

I said, "Yo, this is not like the Chinese food in Harlem. I don't know about this. They do rice here? I thought y'all did rice. Can I get some shrimp or something?"

He said, "Shrimp? No problem. We'll get you some shrimp."

We sit down. We're making small talk through the translator. I'm trying to explain where Harlem is. They're asking me about "The Shammgod." Then the waiter brings out the shrimp, and

I've never seen shrimps like this in my life. These dudes got *fangs*. They so big they got personalities. I swear one looked at me and said, "What's good?"

I'm hallucinating. I'm trying to be polite, so I tell Charles, "Bro, I'm so sorry, but my stomach hurts. I think I caught something on the flight coming over. I'm not real hungry right now."

He's translating to the front-office guys: "Black Man not feel so good."

They're all cracking up.

And listen, don't get me wrong. I'm sure the food was amazing. I'm not hating. But you have to understand, I'm still a raw twenty-two-year-old kid from Harlem. This is all so new to me, and I'm doing it before *anybody* was doing it. Nobody was going overseas to play in China yet. There was no playbook for it. I was the pioneer. I got back to the hotel that night, and I tried to call home, and I didn't realize it was like six o'clock in the morning back in Harlem. Nobody picked up. I was losing it. I called down to the front desk, and I said, "Hello. This is Shammgod. Can somebody in the kitchen make me some chicken fried rice? You know how to do that? No big shrimps. Chicken. Nice little chicken."

I'm looking out of my hotel window down at all the city lights below, just trying to spot a golden arch. I was trippin'.

I couldn't believe it, but thirty minutes later, I get a knock on the door, and they come in with the beautiful silver room service plate, and when I open the lid, I see a perfect chicken fried rice, just like we used to eat in the hood. They gave me a fork and everything. I was so homesick that I could've cried. I've never tasted anything so

good. I told the lady, "Yo, tell the chef thank you. Xiè xiè. *Perfect.*
Thank you, thank you, thank you. Xiè xiè, Xiè xiè."

That chef became my *boy*. He was making me all my favorite
dishes, New York City–style. It was like I had the corner Chinese
joint right in my hotel. My guy was making me beef and broccoli,
egg rolls, everything. The scene in my room every night was ridiculous. They only got three channels on the TV, and one of them
played American TV shows late at night. But for some reason it
was only old shows like *Three's Company* and *The Jeffersons* and *The
Golden Girls*. So picture me: I'm sitting on the bed eating chicken
fried rice, and I'm watching *The Golden Girls*, and it's in English,
but with the Chinese subtitles. It was a hallucination, son.

Blanche, she was always *wildin'*. She was the OG baddie.

Then who was the savage lady? *Dorothy.* You couldn't be messing with Dorothy. She wasn't having it. She'd be arching that
eyebrow, judging you.

It was all I had, so I got so invested. I was watching that show
like it was *The Sopranos*.

My boys used to call me up from Harlem every once in a while,
like "What's good? What you doing over there?"

"I'm just chilling. Eating some eggs rolls. Watching some
Three's Company."

"Yo—what??? You're playing with me."

"For real. They even got *The Jeffersons*."

It was ridiculous. I was counting the days until I could go back
home. But on the court, it was magic.

I played in some exhibition games that first month, and the
fans were going nuts for my dribbling. I couldn't believe how

much they cared about basketball. I was feeling so much love again, like I used to get from the streets, and like I used to get at Providence. It really rejuvenated my passion for the game. The feeling that I used to get when I had a ball in my hands was back. Just that love of the *leather*, son. The feeling of entertaining a crowd. I was back. But still, I missed my family so much. I missed my son. He was walking around now, with his own personality, and I wasn't there. I never wanted him to feel any kind of void in his life, like I felt when I was young. So I got on a flight back to Harlem at the end of the month thinking I'd never go back to China. But that fifty thousand dollars was real. It was in my hands, in cash.

A week later, my agent called me when I was home and said, "If you go back, it's another fifty grand. They *love* you."

I looked at my son, and I knew I couldn't say no. What else am I gonna do? How else we gonna pay for these diapers? I'm not going in the streets. I know how to do one legit thing, and it's play ball. So I got back on the plane and went back to China. And it went down like that literally every single month for the next eight years. I was doing a fifteen-hour flight, almost every month, just to go back to New York to hug my son and my mother and see my boys and recharge my battery.

Then I'd go back to China and be in a whole other world. At home they were calling me a "bust." In China I was a hero. The love was insane. They didn't want to just see me do "The Shammgod." Everything I did—every move, every pass, every bucket, they were going nuts.

And of course, with me being the black Forrest Gump, my path in China led me right into the path of one of the greatest players to ever do it. Right when I first got over there, I kept hearing about this big dude who played in the CBA named "Yow."

I didn't know what people were talking about. Just that "Yow is *nice*. He's huge, but he's so smooth. You gotta see Yow."

I was still so naive that I was thinking to myself: *Yeah, whatever. He's playing in China? He's a Chinese big? Come on, son. How nice can he really be?*

Mannnnn. Joke's on me. The first time I ever saw this dude play, I was amazed. Big fella is 7'6", 300 pounds, and he's out there moving like a ballerina. See, the first thing I always look at in a player is their feet. I don't care if you're a point guard or a center, I'm going straight to the feet. That's how I know if you can really ball, or you're just a pretender. And Yow was *supernice* with the footwork. Smooth. Graceful. He was an artist. They was playing "The Sugar Plum Fairy" whenever Yow had the ball in the post. (Come on, y'all seen *The Nutcracker*.) Yow was *pirouettin'* on dudes.

This man was a *problem*.

That's because Yow was really . . . (Come on, y'all know how this goes.)

Yow was really *Yao Ming*.

Play the man's damn music!!!!!

(Alright, just pretend some dope Chinese music is playing here. I never knew what anything was called. We didn't have no Shazam back then. But they had some bangers with the flutes and everything.)

Before he had any hype in America, Yao was the best player in China. And because it was China, he didn't get *any* special treatment. He's just like everybody else. This man is 7'6" and he's sleeping on two single beds pulled together in the team hotel. That's not a typo. Two *single* beds, with his legs hanging off the edge. I saw it with my own eyes. Yao used to be riding a ten-speed bike to and from practice. A *regular*-sized bike. One of them communist joints with the little basket on the front. He's on that thing looking like a giant, son. It was *stupid*.

But Yao didn't ever complain. He thought it was crazy that *I* thought it was crazy. I'd be talking to him through Charles, hyping him up about how he had to go over to the NBA, and he was really intrigued about everything, like, "In America, you have bigger beds?"

I said, "Yao, we got king size. With the *memory foam*."

He said, "Memory? Foam?"

I said, "Yao, the bed remembers how you be sleeping on it. Very comfortable."

"Interesting."

"And we got a McDonald's on every corner."

"Burgers everywhere?"

"Burgers *everywhere*, Yao."

"And you can eat burgers every day?"

"You can eat 'em for *breakfast*, son."

"Interesting."

He was looking over at Charles like: *Yo, this dude is wild. Where'd they get him from?*

Yao was my *guy*. Yet another kindred spirit that God put in my life. I don't know how a six-foot-tall dude from Harlem and a seven-foot-tall dude from China who don't even speak the same language can be instantly connected like that, but we were. We played against each other in the CBA All-Star Game in 2001, and we almost started a riot. We brought a little bit of the Rucker to the Far East that night. It was late in the game. I was going *off* that night. Yao was going off too. We were putting on a show. Then I had the ball at the top of the key, and I crossed up the defender and drove to the baseline, like I'd done a million times before. But when I got to the rim, all I saw was Yao's huge shadow waiting to swat me. I saw the shadow looming over me before I even looked up. So I just instinctively did a move from the park. I threw the ball between Yao's legs, and it was a piece of cake, because his legs were enormous. I dipped around him and caught the ball on the other side and I did a reverse layup.

The fans were ballistic. They had never seen anything like it. The noise was insane.

That's the moment when I went from "Shammgod" to "God" in China.

The whole building was chanting something, almost like a soccer chant, and I couldn't understand what they were saying. It sounded like, "Gaw-Da! Gaw-Da! Gaw-Da!"

Me and Yao won co-MVP, and when the game was over, I went up to Charles in the locker room and said, "Yo, what were they chanting out there?"

He said, "They were confused. They mixed up the grammar."

"What you mean?"

"They were chanting GOD THE! GOD THE! GOD THE! They were saying you're the God."

"Word?"

"Word. Indeed."

How much money can you put on that memory? These people ain't never seen anything like me before. We don't speak the same language. We come from totally different worlds. But within a year, they totally fell in love with me. And I fell in love with them. China? That's the *homie*. The whole country.

Everywhere I went in China, I was *God-da*.

I was reborn, once again. The money felt good. But the love felt better. The whole experience got me out of my funk. I hadn't had that much fun playing basketball since I was a little kid out at the park.

Every time I was down in the dirt in my life, God gave me another chance. But what people don't understand is, there's no golden light that comes down from heaven. There's nobody playing the harp. Ain't no choir that accompanies a miracle. It's not like God reaches down and gives you a hand. It's more like he talks to you in a whisper, if you know how to listen for it.

He says, "Come this way."

It's on *you* to follow that voice, even if it's to the other side of the globe.

13

You ever seen that old TV show with the homie from *Kill Bill*? From the '70s? *Kung Fu*. David Carradine plays a Shaolin monk, and he's just wandering the earth. He was the reluctant warrior. He was either battling, or he was thinking.

That's how I felt from 2001 to 2008. That was my period of wandering the earth with a basketball in my hand, going from town to town, meeting new people, learning new cultures, and playing for anybody who would pay me in *cash*. When we were on break from the CBA in 2002, I started going to play in these tournaments in Saudi Arabia. The princes and the sheiks over there were crazy about basketball. They used to put on these tournaments all over the Gulf in Dubai and Doha and Riyadh and they'd fly guys in. Of course, because everything in my life seems to lead me into the path of history, you have to remember the timeline. This was a year after the 9/11 attacks, and a year before the invasion of Iraq. Y'all remember the vibes from that time? It was dark. There was so much anti-Islam sentiment in the US, especially in New York City. Maybe it's just my nature, but I never understood it. When the 9/11 attacks happened, I was over in China, and my boys are calling me up in a panic, begging me: "Yo, you gotta come back home right now. Get on the next flight. It ain't safe out there."

And these are some *street* dudes, by the way.

I said, "Wait a minute. Let's think about this. Why would I get on a flight to the US right now? All the planes were going *in that direction*. Maybe y'all should come this way."

Everybody was like, "Huh. Yeah, I guess you're right."

They said, "But aren't you scared over there?"

I said, "Scared of *what*? I almost got killed in Harlem just for looking at a girl's booty. I'm praying for *y'all*."

When I got the chance to go play in Saudi, I looked at it like just another opportunity to grow and to see what was really going on over there, versus what people were saying on TV. I knew from growing up in Harlem that the Harlem that they talk about on the news, or even the Harlem that you see in the movies, it ain't the real Harlem. I wanted to see the real Middle East, even though the bombs were about to start dropping. I grew up in the Muslim faith, and to me, it was always a religion that preached peace above all else. So I took a chance and went to Saudi. From 2002 to 2005, when I was on break from the Chinese league, I played for this team called Al-Ittihad Jeddah.

It was actually a mind-blowing experience to me when I first got there, because I had never been in a country before where my faith was *the* faith. I'm seeing my religion celebrated all over the country, everywhere I go. I'm seeing people stopping from their jobs to pray in the middle of the day. It was such a different experience from America, and everything that our culture holds sacred. Instead of idolizing Gucci and Prada and Nike and Tommy Hilfiger, everybody is just wearing white robes. And it was so funny, because obviously I'm still Shamm from Harlem even though I'm chilling around sheiks, so I'm saying whatever the hell comes to my mind. I'm pointing at their traditional head coverings and I'm like, "Yo, that's dope. You're rocking the red and white picnic table cover. We got that in Harlem! You made the barbecue into a fashion statement, dog. I love it."

They're all laughing.

They're like, "Don't worry, we'll get you one."

Everywhere you went, you saw white robes. After a while, you forgot about fashion and "who got what on." I'm not saying that it's better, I'm just saying it's different. I love Harlem fashion and culture and energy. But to me, Saudi almost felt like a *cleansing*. It was a really deep experience, and it made me question a lot.

I'll never forget, I had this teammate on Al-Ittihad, and he was actually a cousin of Osama bin Laden. The family was super-wealthy and prominent all over Saudi, and he had a lot of cousins, but this guy actually knew him and grew up with him. One day in the locker room, we got to talking about religion and culture and everything—one of those real deep conversations you get into sometimes when you're just killing time in a locker room or on a flight. And I'll never forget, he looked me dead in the eyes, and he said, "You know the biggest difference between us? Americans do everything for money."

Of course, I'm being stubborn. My Harlem is coming out. I'm like, "Nah, nah. That's not true."

He said, "Why are you here?"

I said, "Money."

"Exactly. And what were you just telling me about your friend and his pink car?"

It was hilarious, because right around this time, my boy Cam was finally blowing up as *Cam'ron*. He had just signed a deal with Roc-A-Fella and dropped his first album, and when I went back home to Harlem during one of my breaks, Cam is driving around in the *pink* Range Rover. (He's hanging out the window playing his own song, like, "It's the Boy! I said it's the BOY! OH BOY!")

I said, "Yo, alright. I get your point. We like to flex a little bit. Everybody got their thing. But let's talk about y'all. Y'all really need *four wives*? Come on, son. What's that all about?"

"Well, what do you do in America? You cheat. You lie. You have mistresses. Is that better? Is that a good way to live?"

He's looking at me real hard. He's looking into my *soul*, the way they be doing over there.

"What?"

"Do you know what I'm talking about?"

"No comment."

"*Exactly.*"

"Come on, son. I don't understand how a kid can fly a plane into a building. It just don't make any sense to me."

"Of course you don't understand. Because Americans do everything for money. We do everything for faith."

Damn. I sat with that for a really long time. I'm still sitting with it.

It was such a surreal experience playing over there, because right in the middle of all this conflict and hatred, I'm this black kid from New York City, playing in front of thousands of Muslim dudes in the white robes and the head coverings, and I'm crossing up defenders like I'm at the Rucker, and I'm making the whole crowd go absolutely *nuts*. Picture a wall of white robes, jumping up and down, chanting "Shammgod! Shammgod! Shammgod!" They loved it. They loved me. They were chanting my name from Jeddah to Riyadh to Mecca. What do you say to that? How can you even explain it? If you ever doubted that basketball brings people together, you need to be teleported into a gym in 2003 in Saudi. The United Nations should've hired me, dog. They could've parachuted me into Iraq with a basketball and a Gatorade and I'd have had them signing peace deals within forty-eight hours.

I'll never forget, a member of the Saudi royal family came to one of my games, and I was talking to him afterward, and he said, "What you do with a basketball, it's like Pelé with a football. I've never seen anything like it."

They started paying me year-round to play in Saudi. Almost twenty years before Cristiano Ronaldo was doing it, I was getting the *bag* over there. I was a pioneer, spreading the love of the game for a whole generation of kids, *way* before Neymar and those boys were doing it. But see, my homie was wrong. In the end, he was wrong. We don't do everything for money in America. Just like when I was in China, the money wasn't the whole point. The money was cool. But the love was better. Now I'm getting love in a whole other language. I'm showing the youth that America is not just what *they're* seeing on *their* TV either.

In Saudi, I became a legend. They even painted this huge mural of me in Jeddah, doing my crossover. For me, that's bigger than being in the Hall of Fame. There's about 110 players in the Hall of Fame. How many have a mural in Saudi? How many are called a god in China? How many can go all the way to Africa and have kids coming up to them saying, "You made me play basketball. YouTube. I watched all your highlights."

How many guys only played in twenty NBA games and still became a part of the *culture*?

Still, all good things come to an end. What do they say about Father Time? He's undefeated. It was no different with me. I remember I was about to turn thirty-two, and I just started feeling really tired. Not just physically, but mentally. I'd been overseas for eight years. During that time, I was blessed with two more sons—Eryk and Amir. They were growing up with their mother in Monroe, New York, living that picket-fence suburban life. But I was so busy trying to provide them that life I never had that I was never really there for them, and that was taking its toll on me. We're rich, but we're working rich, you feel me? I got these kids growing up on grass, like I always dreamed life was supposed to be. But we're always one missed check away from going back to concrete. So what do I do? Am I supposed to be a provider? Or am I supposed to be a father? Now I'm having flashbacks to my own father, and my stepfather, and now I'm starting to understand them better. All that tension led to me falling out with their mother, and we were living separately even when I was back in New York. Now I'm just the guy "coming around," like my pops.

Every mistake I said I'd never make . . . Here we are. I'm living it.

The earth spins twice.

Over those eight years, I'd probably taken four hundred flights from Asia to the US and back, just always trying to get that next check. I missed my kids. I was tired of talking to them back home on Skype. Remember that? With the big-ass digital camera clamped to the top of the computer. Connection always going out. Homies turning pixelated. I was so tired of living that Meg Ryan *You've Got Mail* life, you feel me? Finding out about things back home from the little yellow homie. I was tired of going through Customs with money taped to my chest. I was tired of wandering the earth. For the first time in my life, I felt old. I was asking myself what the future held. Can I really be doing this when I'm forty-two? How am I going to support three kids? I was starting to feel a lot of anxiety about the future. I don't know why, but it's like I could hear God whispering to me again. *Come home.*

Then . . . mannnnnn. Guess what happened?

Croatia happened.

You know how it is in the heist movies?

"We got one last job for you."

"Man, I'm *too old for this shit.*"

"Come on, Shamm . . . Just one last job. Piece of cake. It's all mapped out."

It's always that last one that gets you.

Listen man, I'm not hating on Croatia. Let me make that clear. It's a beautiful place and everything. But back in 2008, they were *wildin' out* in Croatia. I won't even say the name of the team I was playing for, because it don't matter. The entire league over there was shady. I heard all the stories about how the Mafia ran things over there.

So when I agreed to go play over there, I told the owner, "Yo, I'll come, but I need my money *up front*. Cash. Before the game."

"Okay. No problem."

Click. I'm on the next flight.

I get over to Croatia, and I'm playing over there for a little bit, and it's all good, but all my teammates are telling me that they haven't been getting paid for months. So we're about to play in this big tournament, and I'm at my apartment two hours before the game, and I'm still waiting for my money. Where's the bagman? Nobody is picking up my calls. I call up one of the front-office guys, and he's telling me, "Don't worry. You'll get your money. It might be a little bit late, but you'll get it."

Nah, now my alarm bells are going off. Something's wrong.

I said, "If I don't have the money in my hand, I'm not playing."

He said, "Alright. Fine. We're coming with your money."

An hour goes by, and I get a knock on my door. The bagman shows up, but it's not like the NBA bagman showing up with the certified check. It ain't even like the Chinese bagman with the crispy bills or the Saudi bagman with the crispy bills and the extra gold watch. No, this was the Croatian bagman. And I'm not trying to be prejudiced or nothing, but the Croatian bagman is looking *exactly* how you're imagining he's looking. Like he's searching for Liam Neeson. So I open the door halfway, and he sticks the bills through the gap—and it's all tens and twenties like we're *doing a drug deal.* He hands me the stripper wad, and he walks off.

Now I'm really thinking: *Something ain't right.* All my Harlem Spidey-senses are going off.

I put the euros in a bag under the bed, with all my other money. It's looking like the currency exchange at the airport up in that joint. I got yuans and riyals and Malaysian money. *I got ringgits, son,* I tell myself. *I got everything. I'm not going to no bank. It's all under the mattress.* So I leave for the game, and something in the back of my mind is also telling me: *Yo, just give the money back and get up out of here.*

Did I give the money back? Did I get up out of there?

Hell naw. I could never say no to a basketball game. So I show up to the game, and everybody from the team is looking at me *crazy.* Real coldblooded. So now I'm talking to one of my European boys on the team, and I'm telling him what happened. And he's like, "You know they come in the night, right?"

I'm like, "Come in the night? *Who* comes in the night, dog?"

He's just nodding like, "Them."

"Son, stop talking all cryptic. *Who?*"

Silence.

"*Who??? Who???* Am I an owl? *Who,* son???"

"Okay," he finally says, "listen. It's a scam. They break into the American players' flats when they're out at the games and they take the money back. They'll say it's just thieves, you understand?"

Now I'm bugging out. I'm looking all around the room at all the coaches and the front-office guys, trying to decipher what's going on. Now all these dudes are looking like Bond villains to me. I'm paranoid. We go out to play the game, and I'm not myself at all. We ended up losing by a bucket at the buzzer, and I ran straight into the locker room, and I didn't even shower. I threw on all my clothes and I got up out of there before anybody else had even untied their shoes. *Zoom.* Cue the movie montage. I speed back to my apartment. *Scrrrrrrrt.* Run inside, go to my bedroom, dive underneath the bed, and I'm feeling around, and . . . my bag is still there. The money is inside. I'm smelling it like it's fresh laundry, man. Praise God. I run into the next room and call up my agent: "Yo, get me on the next flight outta here. I don't care what time. Just the next one."

Click.

I grabbed my piggy bank and my suitcase and I was *gone*. I left pairs of Js and nice jackets all up in that apartment. I didn't care. I flagged down the first taxi I saw.

"Airport. Fast, son. Just go."

Scccrrrrrrrrrrrt.

I'm thinking: *These motherfuckers about to kidnap me if they find me.*

Mannnnn. I'm in the bathroom on the plane taping euros to my chest. I'm thinking: *Yo, I can't be going through Customs with the damn Jason Bourne bag full of funny money. They're gonna call the CIA on me.* So I'm taping $40,000 worth of tens and twenties to my chest, just cursing at myself under my breath, like: *Really, Shamm? You just had to go to Croatia. Had to get that last check. Really, dog?*

Now, remember: This is 2008. We're living in the post-9/11 world. Security was popping everywhere. My passport is looking *crazy*. I'm a thirty-two-year-old black man named God Shamm-god. I got stamps from Saudi Arabia, the Emirates, Malaysia, China . . . You think I'm just gonna skate through the border with Officer McGilicutty looking through my papers? Nah, son. We land at JFK Airport in New York and I got *forty thou* in small-money euros taped up under my hoodie, and I'm just looking at all those Customs officers in the stalls like: *Please, God. Please just give me the friendliest motherfucker you got. Please just smile on me today, Lord.*

I'm near the front of the line, and I'm psychoanalyzing all these agents. I see one on the end that's looking real promising. Homegirl. Real New Yorker. Maybe I can smooth-talk her . . .

Anything to declare?

Yeah, you're looking real fly today.

But do I get homegirl down at the end? Nope. Of course not. I get the real military-looking crew-cut homeboy a few stalls down. He's wagging that militant finger at me, like: *This way, son.*

Oh *hell naw*. I'm going to jail. I'm done. I spent thirty-two years on this earth dodging this fate, and now I'm going to jail over the *Euroleague*. This can't be my life, son. The walk to that stall felt like it took ten years. I'm studying the dude's face. I'm looking for any sign of suspicion. And I feel like he's definitely looking at me *funny*. He's squinting a little bit.

I get up to the glass with that little peephole, and he says, "Passport."

No hello. No "how was your trip." Just . . . *passport*.

I slide that thing under the glass, and I'm already thinking about who I still know who might be locked up in Rikers Island. I'm wondering how the food is gonna be. He's flicking through my passport with the *fury*. He's flicking through every page, and he don't like what he's seeing. You know when they stop on a page and they just freeze on it? He's freezing on every page. He's shaking his head.

I'm bugging.

He looks up from the passport.

He's looking at me.

He looks down at it again.

Looks back at me.

"*Shammgod?*"

"Yes?"

Big-ass smile.

"*God* Shammgod. No way. It's really you?"

"It's really me."

"I'm a big fan, man. Nobody got handles like you. Where you coming from?"

"Croatia."

"Croatia!"

"Yes, sir."

"Well, *I'll be!*"

We were standing there talking about basketball for what seemed like ten minutes.

"Man, I wished the Knicks would've drafted you . . . Well, *anyway*! Welcome home!"

He waved me through.

For the 417th time, my handle saved my damn life.

(And yes, for any feds who might be reading this, I did deposit that cash into an FDIC bank account and yes I did pay my taxes. Chill.)

I got home and I went to sleep, and when I woke up the next morning, I went on Yahoo Messenger.

Bing, bing, bing, bing.

My away message had been popping off. I'm getting lit up with a million messages, all at once.

I click onto the one from my American teammate who is still back in Croatia.

BasketballrSwish23: YO!!!! WHERE ARE YOU?!?!?!?

BasketballrSwish23: hey please tell me where r u

BasketballrSwish23: bro you gotta call me they r here i think

BasketballrSwish23: yup they at the door . . . they r looking for you

BasketballrSwish23: OH SHIT THEY ARE KICKING MY DOOR IN!!!!!!!

BasketballrSwish23: bro

BasketballrSwish23: they kicked my front door down dog. . . . they say they wanna talk to you. LOL. They said they been to your apartment and ur not there

BasketballrSwish23: bro if you don't come home im pretty sure they r gonna kill yo ass!!!!! LOL

I replied.

Shammgod12: sup?

. . . Bing.

BasketballrSwish23: Yo!!!! Where you at???

Shammgod12: I'm in harlem.

BasketballrSwish23: harlem??? LOL. They tore your whole place up.

Shammgod12: word?

BasketballrSwish23: hey, can i give u a piece of advice?

Shammgod12: ya?

BasketballrSwish23: don't ever come back to Croatia dog!!!! your face is gonna be on the milk cartons

(Shammgod12 has signed off.)

I shut the computer down. And that was a wrap. On everything. I made up my mind that I was done running around the world chasing paper. My oldest son was fourteen years old. He was about to start playing high school basketball. Guess where? In the same gym he was raised in, of course. My alma mater, La Salle Academy. I spent most of my life trying to make sure that he would never have to worry about a thing. But he needed a father who was actually going to be there in the stands at his games. He needed a father who actually had a future. He didn't need the legend. He needed the human being.

I just remember shutting the computer down and just sitting there in silence, thinking:

Alright. I gave twenty years of my life to this game. What now? Talk to me, God. What is my higher calling?

God was silent.

I meditated on it for days.

Nothing. Months went by. I was lost.

For a whole year, I didn't hear a thing.

For the first time in my life, since I was lying on that bench, praying for a miracle, I had no direction.

I was out on the block in Harlem when I almost got killed for the fourth time in my life. I was thirty-three. In hood years, that's seventy-three. I'm still young, but I already lived three lifetimes. I had a fourth son, Prince, on the way. So a *whole lot* of money is coming out, and all of a sudden, nothing is coming in. I'm looking at these kids, like, "Man, y'all better be mixing up that protein powder. I'm six-foot-flat with Pumas on. Y'all gonna need some *scholarships* in this house."

I still had some overseas money saved up, but it was dwindling. It's not like now, where the NBA deals are so crazy that you can be the eleventh man on the bench for a year and be making $17 trillion. Dudes shooting be 15 percent from three and be making generational wealth out here now. I made *Kia* money, son. I couldn't even buy my momma a condo with my rookie deal. *And* I walked five miles to school in the snow. (Y'all soft!!)

Anyway, the long and the short of it is: I was in a predicament. I have a fifteen-year-old son at home, and this boy is *eating*. I got grocery bills to pay and no checks coming in. No college degree.

No 401(k). Definitely can't be a hustler. *Dang.* I didn't know what to do with my life. I was lost. So I did what I always do when I feel lost. I went to hang out with the same people I grew up with.

A lot of my old friends, they were still back in Harlem. I went to see my boy Howie, and we went to a block party on 142nd Street, right around the corner from the building I grew up in. Right around the corner from where me and Mase got robbed fifteen years before. And I hadn't learned anything. I did the dumbest thing you can do when you got a little money and a lot of fame. I wore all my jewelry to the block party.

Yo, a little word to the wise . . . If you learn nothing from this book, just remember this one little thing, and it might save your life: don't wear all your chains to the cookout, son.

Don't be like me. Leave the chains at home.

I don't know *who* I was trying to be at thirty-two years old, but I showed up rocking two chains and a gold watch. To eat *burgers*, son. On 142nd Street. Who am I even stunting on? My auntie? My boys from the sixth grade? *Stupid.*

It was so weird, because the entire time I was at the party, I felt this *weight* on my chest. It literally felt like my chains were heavy. I couldn't breathe right. I felt ridiculous. I kept making jokes the whole time to my boys, like, "Yo, why am I rocking two chains? We used to make fun of dudes like me. Grown-ass man out on the block in his jewelry."

Something was off. Even the watch on my wrist felt tight. I kept loosening the neck on my shirt. I wanted to take everything off. I felt hot.

I said, "Yo, imagine Gregg Popovich coming out of the tunnel rocking the Cuban links. I guess I need to retire all the jewelry, huh? I got three kids and another one on the way, man. What am I doing with all this?"

It was like I had a premonition. I'm walking home from the cookout with my boy Howie at two o'clock in the morning. We're on 142nd and 8th Avenue when a car pulls up on us. Creeps. Stops. All the doors open up at the same time. Six dudes jump out, rocking the sheisties. This ain't my first rodeo. When are the guns coming out?

The guns come out.

"Yo, Shammgod!"

Alright, this is new. They know who I am.

"We know who you are. We know where your family lives. Don't run, nigga."

The guy in front of me put a gun to my forehead.

Two dudes on the sides put guns to my ribs.

Two dudes got guns on Howie.

"Give us everything or we'll kill you right now."

I looked down at my watch, and I had this flashback to me and Mase getting robbed when we were eighteen right in this same spot. Back then, we had our whole lives ahead of us. I remembered how he threw the watch like we were in a movie, and how we ran up out of there and flagged down the NYPD. But I wasn't eighteen no more. And life isn't a movie. I was tired, man. Tired of running. Tired of the streets. Tired of my chains. Tired of everything.

I said, "Bro, you can have it all. Nobody gotta die today over a chain."

They were trying to yank my chain over my head, but it had a double lock on it, and I said, "Yo, relax. I'll take it off for you. I don't want it anyway."

They lowered the guns, and I took all my shit off and handed it over to them.

"Enjoy it."

They were looking at one another like, *Yo, this is the weirdest robbery ever.*

The craziest part was, I knew exactly who was robbing me. It was a setup. In five minutes, I could've gone back to the party and called up some muscle and got the chains back. I could've done a whole lot more to those boys too. With a snap of a finger, I could've gotten some street justice. But I've seen exactly where that leads. You know where it leads? Nowhere. It's a circle. Revenge never ends. Just keeps going round and round.

I needed an ending. I needed a new chapter.

When they got in the car and sped off, me and my boy Howie did what you always do when you get robbed. You sit on the sidewalk and you stare into space for ten minutes.

Howie was sobbing. He was like, "Yo, that was nuts. Six dudes. What the fuck. I'm too old for this shit. We almost got killed over some *bullshit.*"

He had snot bubbles coming out.

I just started cracking up.

He's looking at me like, "Yo, what the fuck is so funny?! We almost *died*!"

I said, "But we alive."

"Yeah, we alive . . ."

"WE ALIIIIIIIIIVE!!!"

"Bro, what's wrong with you?"

"YO WE ALIIIIIIIIIIIVE!!! AHAHAHAHAHA!!! YO!!! I TOLD YOU, SON!!! AHAHAHAHA!!!"

I was out of my mind. I was smelling the air like I never smelled New York City air before. I was looking up at the buildings like I had never seen public housing before. I was about to do snow angels on the sidewalk. I could've hugged a pigeon, bro. I was so happy to be alive.

I wasn't just alive, I was reborn.

I said, "I told you, bro. I had a feeling. God was sending me a message. I had to let go. I just had to let go. . . ."

Howie was looking at me like I had lost my damn mind.

Maybe I had. But I never felt better.

I went to see my mom the next day, and I told her, "Remember how I always promised you I'd finish my degree? I'm going back to school."

She said, "Wow, really?"

"Really."

"Can I ask a stupid question, baby?"

"Yeah?"

"You're not gonna be mad at me?"

"No! What's up?"

"Do they let you back into college at *thirty-three*?"

"If you're Shammgod, I think they do."

"Okay . . . Well, that's nice, baby."

So at thirty-three years old, I called up Providence, and they let me reenroll as an undergraduate. I packed everything I owned into my SUV and I drove up to Rhode Island. Nothing on the campus had changed. Same buildings. Same smell. Same sweatshirts. Even some of the professors were the same. The only thing that was different was the music. They weren't rocking Hootie and the Blowfish in 2010. I was walking to class on the first day, with my backpack and all my books—and yo, the books got *mad expensive*, by the way—and some of the students and the teachers were doing double takes like, *Wait a minute . . . Is that . . . Nah . . . Is it?*

When I did college the first time, I didn't care about nothing but basketball. I was in the *way* back of the classroom, in the paper airplane section, if I showed up at all. But the second time, I did the opposite. I had no choice. These books are all I *got* now. I just paid the bookstore $557 for an *economics* book? I gotta be getting my money's worth. So now I'm sitting in the front of the class like the valedictorian. I'm thirty-three years old, and I'm that annoying dude scribbling notes on everything the teacher is saying. Now *I'm* the poor motherfucker I used to hit in the back of the head with the paper planes. I'm nerding out, son.

It took like one class before one of the other students whispered to me: "Are you . . . are you . . . Shammgod?!"

They were all looking at me like: *Aren't you like . . . a millionaire? What are you doing here?*

They had no idea that at the end of every night, I went back to my SUV, and I threw my bookbag in the trunk, and I reclined the front seat all the way back, and I slept in my car.

I didn't have money for an apartment. I didn't have the heart to ask for student housing. It never came up. They probably thought I was living in a mansion off campus. I started helping out with the basketball team—nothing paid, just for credit—and I would go early in the morning and use the showers after I worked out. I still had fly clothes and Jordans and a big smile on my face, so nobody could have imagined that I was struggling.

After about a month, I was sleeping in the car one night, parked right around the corner from the arena, when I heard a tap on the window. That flashlight tap. Everybody in the hoods knows that. I rolled down the window.

"Good evening, Officer. Is there a problem?"

"You okay out here?"

"Oh yeah, I'm cool. We just had a late practice and I was so tired that I took a nap. I'll be out of here in a minute."

"Okay . . . Have a good night."

Two nights later, another tap on the window. Same security guard.

"Awww, my bad, Officer. I just . . ."

"No problem. Just checking you're alright."

"All good. All good . . ."

He flashed the light into the back seat, and all my clothes were piled up back there. Socks, underwear, everything. He didn't say anything. He just gave me a nod and walked away. The next day, I got a call from the school administration. As soon as I saw the number, I thought they were going to kick me out of school. I picked up the phone ready to give them some nonsense, but they didn't say anything about me sleeping in my car. They just said, "Hi, Mr. Shammgod. Just letting you know that there must have been a mix-up with your housing. We have a dorm room for you. It's ready to go. You can move in tomorrow."

"Oh . . . Thank you."

(And if that security guard happens to be reading this: *Thank you.*)

At thirty-three years old, I moved into a regular dorm on campus. Everything you're picturing is exactly how it was: The wooden bed frame. That *light* wood. The plastic mattress cover. The community shower with the shower *flip-flops*. Oh yeah, dog. A real dorm. They must have felt bad for me, because they hooked me up with a double room for just one person. So there were actually *two* double beds in there, and I pushed them together to make a king-size bed in the middle of the room. In the hood, we improvise. We always find a way. So I went to Bed Bath & Beyond and got the king-size memory foam cover to put over top of both beds, right? To create a seal. But it never really worked right, and in the middle of the night if I moved around too much, I'd be sinking into the bottomless *pit* in the middle of the beds. And it was like quicksand. The more you tried to get out, the more you *sunk back in*. I'd be trapped in there at four o'clock in the morning, staring up at the ceiling like, *Yo, is this real? I'm a father. I played in the NBA. I got a mural in the Middle East. How is this my life?*

Ridiculous. But I loved it. I was living that true sophomore life. I was cleansed. I was stripped of everything. Everything but my Bed Bath & Beyond candles, son. My room was smelling like a million bucks. The best part was the cafeteria and the meal plan.

Oh my God, man. I was in heaven. I forgot how good it was to be eating three meals a day at the cafeteria. I didn't appreciate it the first time around. I felt like I was in high school again. I'd be sitting in class just daydreaming with my stomach growling, like, *Man, I wonder if they're gonna have the chicken nuggets today for lunch. I hope they got nuggets with the little crispy tater tots.*

And we're not even talking about the *drinks*, man. The drinks they had in there were heavenly. The *cran-apple juice*, son? I would go in there in the morning and get four of them and put them in my bag for the day. If I got a meal card in my pocket, I'm in heaven. I'm *set.*

Every little dollar I had extra, I was sending it home to my family. So I ate every meal in that cafeteria. I was so locked in that all I used to do for fun was go to the movies on the weekend. Other than that, I was either in class or in the gym, helping the team. It's kind of crazy, but you'd be surprised how little college teams were working on ball handling at the time. Even now. It's not really something with specialized coaches. So I saw an opportunity, and I made it my specialty. I would look for the guys on the team who were really hungry—who really wanted to be great— and I would offer to train them for an hour after practice just on their handle. Same as me and Kobe back in the day. We're not putting *no* shots up. We're just dribbling till we drop. And I'm doing it right with you. We're not stopping until we're two sweat puddles on the floor.

It got to the point where the dudes on the team just loved being around me and laughing at all my stories from my life, so even if they hated dribbling and hated my workouts, they used to come and suffer anyway, just to hear my stories. And I'll never forget the way the vibe changed with some of the coaches. I know how it is in locker rooms. It's very complicated. Because once you become the coach that the players want to be around, there can be a lot of jealousy and paranoia.

It wasn't like I came back to Providence to revolutionize the program. It was more like, *Alright, cool. You can help out.*

The coaches started making little comments like, "Oh yeah, we know Shamm got his little workouts. But we're here to do the *real* work."

Man, I was just happy to be there. Happy to be sweating in a gym. Happy to have a purpose. I wasn't trying to take anybody's job. And I'll never forget, we lost a tough game one night and we were in the locker room afterwards, and the coach is trying to give everybody a kick in the ass with his speech. One of my jobs was to pick up the used towels and the Gatorade bottles and the tape and everything. So that's what I was doing, while he was ripping into the team.

Then he pointed to me in the middle of his speech, and he said, "Look at him. Is that what you want to be? You want to be thirty-three years old and picking up towels?"

You could've heard a pin drop in there.

I just stopped and looked at him.

Everybody probably thought I was going to kill him.

But I didn't react at all. I bent down and picked up another towel, and I put it in the bin. Picked up another towel, put it in the bin.

He finished his speech, and as soon as he left the room, all the guys turned to me and were trying to big me up.

"Man, he don't know what he's talking about, bro."

"Don't worry about it, Shamm."

"We got you, dog."

I said, "I'm not worried about a thing. I'm doing what I love. He was trying to deliver a message, and it just came out wrong. We all got a job to do."

I finished picking up the towels. That was it. But that was probably the single most important moment of my life. Because if I had let my ego get the best of me and I had blown up, I wouldn't be living the life I am now. He would have been exactly right about me. I would be somewhere else right now, probably still picking up towels. Maybe worse. Maybe not here at all.

I could've snapped. I could've let my pride get the best of me. I could've walked through the wrong door.

Instead, I walked through Door No. 2. Instead, I'm an NBA coach.

I let my ego die so that I could really live.

From that day on, I had the loyalty of everybody in that room. They would've walked through a brick wall for me. I kept chipping away, and eventually they actually let me sit on the bench with the coaching staff. I still picked up towels sometimes, but I became an official assistant coach. One of the guys I was working one-on-one with every day was Kris Dunn. He was the first McDonald's All-American to come to Providence since a kid from Harlem named Shammgod. He actually grew up watching tapes of me when he was a little kid, and we formed an instant bond.

Kris was always a supremely talented guard, but once we really started working together, his game started taking off. His junior year, in 2015, he blew up and won Big East Player of the Year, and it was the same deal as me when I blew up in '97. He had all these agents telling him that he should go into the draft and make millions. But Kris came from a solid family, and I got really close to his parents, and I knew that they wanted him to come back for his senior year and get his degree.

They asked me what I thought. And the thing about me is that the only person I ever want to be in life is *me*. I'm always going to be Shammgod. I'm not gonna be your hype man. I'm not gonna try to be your agent or your right-hand man. I'm always gonna tell you the absolute truth, like the Master Sensei Kevin Jackson always told me. See, I never had a big brother or a father when I was growing up who could guide me. I never even had anybody in my life who I could really talk to about the business of basketball. At least I didn't have anybody that was going to give me the hard truth.

When I wasn't sure whether to stay in school or declare for the NBA Draft, you know what everybody told me?

"Yeah, you should come out. Come out, come out, come out."

And you know what those same people told me when I got released?

"Mannnnn, you should've stayed one more year."

So when I got close to Kris and some other guys at Providence, I was trying to be that older brother for them. The guy who would never pull any punches, you feel me?

So when his parents asked me what he should do, I said, "He shouldn't make the same mistake I did. I should've been a lottery pick. But I gave in to my fears. If he goes in the draft now, he's probably a second round pick. If he comes back, I think he can be Top Ten."

I made his parents a promise.

I said, "If he comes back, I promise you that I will get your son to the NBA."

And what did he do? He came back.

That 2015–16 season, a really crazy thing happened. Another divine intervention. Kobe Bryant had announced his retirement, and it was like the entire basketball world stopped for a whole season to give this man his flowers. It was amazing. Kobe was finally smiling with everybody, and just enjoying life and letting it all sink in. He was giving an interview with a reporter, and they were asking him about when he was a teenager, and he said something to the effect of "You know who taught me how to dribble right? Shammgod."

"Who?"

"Shammgod."

People had no idea that we even knew each other, let alone that we were boys. Dudes on the team were coming up to me like, "Yo, you really knew *Kobe*? For real?"

I said, "You thought I was just a towel boy? Come on, son."

I never threw anybody's name around. I never told anybody my stories unless they asked me. All of a sudden, people are looking at me differently. Everybody is asking me if I can train them in the summer, even guys in the NBA. You have to understand: When I came to Providence, we hadn't made March Madness in almost ten years. Then we made it in back-to-back-to-back seasons, and everybody started paying attention to what we had going on up in Rhode Island. I was just a small part of that success, but I was a part of it, and that meant the world to me.

One day, I was doing my normal after-practice workout with Kris. At that point, NBA scouts were starting to come around all the time. I didn't really pay them no mind. We had our heads down. But then one day, Michael Finley walks into the gym. And Mike, that's another one of my *guys*. Mike was shooting the lights out for the Dallas Mavericks when I was in the league. Then he kept shooting the lights out for the Spurs and helped them win the title in 2007. I hadn't seen him in a long time, but I knew that he had just started coaching for the Mavs. He came into the gym and dapped me up and we started talking, and he said, "Yeah, Mike Procopio saw what you were doing with these guys up here and he said it was amazing. I had to come see for myself."

Mike Procopio was Kobe's longtime personal coach. He started doing some work for the Mavs in player development, and he came to scout one of our players named Ricky Ledo the first year I got to Providence, when I was still living out of my car. The craziest part about it is that Ricky Ledo got hit with a Prop 48 violation as a freshman. He didn't have enough high school credits to be academically eligible, and the NCAA wouldn't let him play. Ricky was a local kid from Providence, the No. 1 player in the state, and they almost ruined his life. Now these college kids are getting penthouses paid for by NIL money, but back in 2012, they kept this kid off the court over some damn *home economics* credits or whatever. It was crazy.

Ricky couldn't even practice with the team, so I started working him out myself, one-on-one. The dude was so talented that the Mavs sent Mike Procopio to come scout Ricky, and we lit the gym on fire. The Mavs drafted the kid in the second round without him even having played a single college game. I remember Mike saying, "Man, you should be doing this in the NBA."

He never forgot about me. He kept telling Michael Finley and all the player development guys at the Mavs that they had to come see what I was doing with these kids. So once Kris Dunn was getting hype, they came around again.

Finley and the Mavs scouts watched me and Kris do our *nutso* workout for an hour, and then he dapped me up again and left. I didn't think anything of it. Two weeks later, I got a phone call.

It was Mark Cuban.

What did I tell you about the world? It spins twice. See, I actually played a few games for the Mavericks Summer League team before I went to China. It didn't work out, but Mark really liked my game, and he really liked my personality, and he never forgot about me.

Mark said, "Shammy! Remember me? Listen, I keep hearing about all these great things you're doing with these kids at Providence. We want to fly you down to Dallas to talk to you."

I said, "Word?"

He said, "Absolutely!"

So I flew down to Dallas and I met with Mark for a few hours, and he basically offered me a job on the spot as the NBA's first-ever ball handling coach. I mean, remember: I'm still living in a dorm room, and this man is offering me a stable job making six figures, flying on the PJ with the catered breakfast, lunch, and dinner and the good health insurance? Are you serious?

What do you think I said?

I said *no*.

"Sorry, but I can't do it."

I don't think Mark was used to hearing no like that, especially from somebody living in a dorm.

He said, "Are you sure? I can't promise you that the job is going to be here next season."

I said, "Look, I promised a kid that I was going to help him live his dream. I gave my word."

I know everybody says that basketball is just a business. But to me, it's a lot more than that. It's an extension of life itself. And in life, you always have to trust your gut, right? Every time you ignore your gut, you end up playing yourself. When they offered me the job, I just had this flashback to when I was coming out of school, and I made the decision to go to the NBA without my full heart being in it. I made myself a promise that I'd never rush my process or betray my principles ever again. My word is bond. Period.

I put my trust in God and I told Mark I had to stay.

That was the beginning of a lifelong friendship between me and him.

I got back on the plane and I flew back to campus. And you know what the craziest part is? At this point in time, I had *roommates*. My boy Howie—the same Howie I grew up with, the same Howie I got robbed with—he ran into some trouble in Harlem, and he needed to get up out of there for a minute. And my other boy Woods, he needed a new start too. Remember him from playing Manhunt back in the day? We were all still tight after all these years. So I told them to come up to Providence and live with me for a while until things settled down. At that point, I had gotten upgraded to one of the bigger dorms, and we were able to finesse three beds in there.

Picture it: You got three thirty-something Harlem dudes stuffed into this dorm room. On one side you got their bunk beds, and on the other side you got my bed, and then on the back wall you just got like three hundred boxes of Nike and Reebok and Puma and Adidas and Tims. Even when I wasn't getting money, I was always getting free shoes. They were my prized possessions and I brought them all up to school with me. So we had them all stacked up against the back of the room like a multicolored Great Wall of China. If you were just some random engineering student walking by and we happened to open the door, it was probably looking like the *trap house* in there. But we weren't really doing anything except watching basketball and kung fu movies and chilling like we were kids again. It was amazing, man. I was broke, but I was having the time of my life.

A couple weeks later, my boy Jason Wingate hit me up, and he was looking to start a new chapter too. Jason was a Rucker

Park legend. They called him J5. He had just wrapped up a career overseas, and he heard what we had going on up in Providence, and he said, "Man, you mind if I stay with you for a minute?"

I said, "Why not? Come on up. Get in where you fit in. That's the Harlem way."

So we added a fourth homie. We were like a full *frat* almost. We should've put the Greek letters on the front door. J5 came up with a backpack and a pillow and he was staying with us for a while, until he got a job coaching at a local high school.

If you only live for money, you're going to be spiritually broke. At Providence, in the dorms with my childhood friends, laughing about old stories from back in the day, eating chicken nuggets for dinner every night, going to the gym every morning at six o'clock, reheating burritos in the microwave of the coach's room, just following the path that God had put in front of me . . . Son, I really felt like a billionaire. When my head hit the pillow at night, I was at peace for maybe the first time in my life.

That spring, I graduated from Providence College, twenty years after I enrolled as a freshman. *With honors*, son. I got the whole cap and gown moment, like in the movies. It was one of the most euphoric moments of my life. Not because of anything I did. I just did what I was supposed to do two decades prior. Nah, that day wasn't about me. It was the greatest moment of my life, other than the birth of my children, because I knew my mother was in the crowd watching me. I had made a promise to her, and I kept it. She had so many struggles in her life, but she was a beautiful soul. She was the epitome of the expression, "Don't expect nothing, but appreciate everything."

I remember when five minutes after I got drafted into the NBA, everybody was still hugging and talking about how big my checks were gonna be, my mom had already disappeared back in the kitchen.

"Momma, what you doing?"

"Somebody gotta make these chicken wings."

"Mom, come on."

"You want to eat, or what?"

That was her in a nutshell. She fed my friends when we were down to the last box of mac 'n' cheese. A hard life, but a pure soul.

She deserved that moment, seeing her son throw his cap up into the air.

God Shammgod belongs to the culture.

Shammgod *Wells* belongs to my mother.

And now Mr. Wells, her baby boy, was a college graduate.

When I found her after the ceremony and gave her a hug, I said, "See? I promised you. Don't I always keep my promises?"

She cried tears of joy. She cried harder than when I got drafted, for real.

That was an incredible year. I got upgraded to the graduate dorms, and I felt like I was living like a king. That was like the Providence penthouse. The university gave me a $16,000 stipend for this graduate program I was in, and I took $8,000 and sent it to my kids, and I took the other $8,000 and I bought the *flyest* broke-ass car I could find on the lot. It was a BMW 7-Series with like seven-hunnid-million miles on it. I pulled up to practice, and all my players were saying, "Bro, you gotta let me drive that thing up to the party this weekend. Where'd you get the money for that?"

They really thought I was a millionaire again.

What they didn't know was, me and Howie and Woods and J5 are driving this thing back to New York over a holiday break, and it's *smoking*. We had to stop on the side of the road every thirty miles and let the engine cool off. It took us ten hours to get back to Harlem instead of three, but we were laughing the whole way. We were really ready to die for looking fly. That's the Harlem way. Lord, let me go up in smoke. I don't even care. As long as I don't go out looking *broke*.

We're sitting there waiting for the car to turn back on, and it's making that choking noise, and my boys are looking at me like, "Yo, you could've been in the *NBA*, dummy. What are we doing?"

I'm cracking up.

"You think we got enough gas money to get back to Harlem? We might have to take the bus."

I mean, what am I gonna do? Cry? You gotta laugh, man. I used to be *Shammgod*. I used to have sheiks giving me private tours of diamond mines in the Middle East. Now I'm sitting on the side of the Bronx Expressway and my BMW is turning into a *s'more*, dog.

That was a year that I'll never forget, for as long as I live. It was just *pure*. No matter how much money you make, you can never get those times back. "Remember when" ain't for sale. Remember that, son.

At the end of that season, in June 2016, I fulfilled another important promise.

"With the fifth pick in the 2016 NBA Draft, the Minnesota Timberwolves selected . . . Kris Dunn from Providence College."

I told his parents he'd go Top 10, if he stuck with me.

He went Top 5.

Seeing the Dunn family crying tears of joy, it took me back to that night when my name got called, and everything that I ever dreamed about came true. But honestly? I felt even more fulfilled helping somebody else fulfill their dreams. I could feel a deep sense of purpose that night.

The grasshopper was finally becoming the sensei, you feel me?

I could hear God speaking to me again. I knew my purpose. It was written.

A few days later, Mark Cuban called me up.

"Okay, Shammy. You ready now?"

Seventeen years after I walked out of my coach's office without saying a word, rocking a durag and some Tims, not knowing where my life was heading or how I was going to feed my family, I was walking back into an NBA building through the front door. This time as a coach. This time as a *teacher*.

How can you even explain that?

It all comes back around.

The earth spins twice.

15

Not too many people get a real second act in this life. I got four of 'em. I told you, my life is not normal. It's Shakespearean, son.

Act 1, I was Shammgod Wells, the man.

Act 2, I was God Shammgod, the myth.

Act 3, I was a *God-da*, the legend.

Then, when I had been stripped of all my pride and my earthly possessions . . . when I was down to my last dollar . . . when I was back to eating chicken wings for dinner . . . when my life had come full circle . . . I was reborn again.

In Act 4, I simply became "Coach Shamm." Not a man, a myth, or a legend, but a humble teacher.

I got the chance to follow in the footsteps of all the men who gave a damn about me in my life: KC, Tiny Archibald, Thurman Player, Kevin Jackson, Ron Carlos, and a lot of guys in the hood you've never read about in the papers.

When somebody helps you like Mark Cuban helped me, your only job is to make them look like a genius. My first day of work at the Mavs felt like the first day of school, man. I was so nervous to make a good impression, and you already know *I don't get nervous.* But that's when I got a basketball in my hand. When I got *khakis* on? That's a different story. First day, I came so overdressed that dudes were looking at me funny. I met with Mark, and he told me, "Just be you. Don't try to be anybody else. I hired you to be Shamm."

Think about it. What did you do on the first day at your job? Did you set up your email address? Did you have some cupcakes in the lunchroom? Yo, on my first day at work, I was guarding *Dirk Nowitzki.* That was my orientation, son. And it was so funny, because I didn't expect Dirk to be talking any shit. But Dirk was talking *mad shit,* in his own way.

He's seven feet. I'm six feet. I'm like a little pit bull just nipping at his heels, trying to do anything I can do to knock him off balance, and he's just backing me down into the post, *laughing* his Dirk laugh.

He's like, "You too little."

I'm like, "Man, you too old!"

"We're the same age. Only you're *little.*"

Then he hits me with the one-leg turnaround fadeaway. The Dirk Special. Seen it ten thousand times on TV. In person, it's unguardable. Splash.

"Too small. Go sit down."

"Man, come on, Dirk. Let's work on your handle, big fella."

"Anybody can dribble."

"See, you *right.* But I'm not gonna teach you how to dribble. I'm gonna teach you *handle.*"

"I can already do the Shammgod."

"Mannnnnnnn . . ."

"Watch me! Watch me!"

He was like a little kid.

"Dirk, you thirty-seven years—"

"Watch me!"

Then he did the slowest, most *Dirk* version of the Shammgod I've ever seen, and he stepped back and shot a perfect three. Splash. It looked like it hurt his back just to do it. But he had to show me that he could pull it off, as an homage to the culture.

This thirty-seven-year-old German dude . . . one of the best to ever play the game . . . and still the Shammgod meant something to him.

It was one of the coolest moments of my life. I'd seen so many players do the Shammgod on TV over the years. Chris Paul, Russell Westbrook, Damian Lillard, Jamal Crawford, Allen Iverson, Ja Morant . . . It's always amazing to see. But to see it in person, as a coach, with a guy who grew up so far outside our culture, but who still wanted to show love to it anyway, that's a memory I'll take with me to the afterlife, man.

I told Dirk, "Man, I'm gonna give you the highest compliment I can give a player. You *old as hell*, and you're still working like you're twenty-one."

From that day on, me and Dirk were boys.

If I have any secret as a coach, it's that there is no secret. I'm just *me*. I treat every player in the NBA the same as I treated my players at Providence, and the same as I treated any of my boys at Rucker Park. If you're calculating, you're *faking*. If you want your words to carry weight, you need to be 100 percent you, even if what you're saying hurts.

I'm not Coach K. I'm not Gregg Popovich. I've lived a very different life. But that don't make my wisdom any less deep. My mission was to take everything that I learned in the streets and the parks and the gyms from Harlem to Madison Square Garden to Kuwait and pay it forward to this new generation. Because let's be honest, man, these kids *need* some help. They got what you call one of them *good* problems. They're *too* rich. They got so much money that they can't see *over* it. They don't know what's on the other side. They're in a green prison. Then they wake up one morning wondering why they're not happy. Why basketball is a stress and not an escape. Why they're not achieving greatness. Dog, because you're so rich that everybody around you is *lying* to you. They're telling you what you want to hear. My job was to bring a little bit of reality into the mix. A little bit of Harlem down to Dallas.

Honesty. People aren't used to it. If you got over $6 million in a checking account, you're probably never gonna hear honesty the rest of your damn life.

I'll never forget, we had Frank Ntilikina on our team, and he was a really talented player and a really good kid. But he was one of those lottery picks from France who come over to the NBA and have a hard time finding their lane. He came over to us from the Knicks as our backup point guard, and he was struggling. One day after practice, we get to talking, and Frank asked me an honest question.

He said, "Coach Shamm, do you think I'm looking selfish when I'm out there on the court?"

So I gave him an honest answer.

I said, "Well, I don't know if you're selfish or not. But I know you be out there taking some *crazy-ass* shots."

He just stopped for a minute and was looking at me like he got punched in the stomach. He was frozen.

He said, "Man, you really just said that to me?"

I said, "Yeah. You look crazy. What do you want me to say?"

He just started cracking up, like, "Damn. You're right."

The worst sin you can ever commit is to lie to *yourself*. The problem is, you only learn that lesson after you lie to yourself long enough to realize it. Frank knew that I was coming from a place of complete humbleness. You think I wasn't out on an NBA court looking crazy sometimes? You think I wasn't delusional, at twenty years old? You think I never *played myself*? Come on, son. I made a million mistakes. But I never failed. You can never fail if you learn from it and keep moving forward.

Still, I was taking a risk by being me.

I was still the "streetball" guy. I couldn't shake that stigma. I was the Harlem dude. I didn't talk like other coaches. And I was coming into the building on the lowest rung on the ladder— as a player development coach with a focus on ball handling, which was unheard of at that time. The easiest thing for me to do would've been to be "the homie." Every NBA locker room got one. That's the player's coach. That's the guy everybody vents to, and he's like a mirror. "Yep. You right, you right, you right. Coach should be playing you more. Yep, you right. The media be acting crazy. You right, man."

He never goes left. It's always "right, right."

But my thinking was, you're always one phone call away. You're one phone call away from getting hired, and you're one phone call away from getting fired. So you might as well be honest, because eventually, your ass is gonna get fired anyway.

One of the first things I did was I started working one-on-one every day with Harrison Barnes. That's like my little brother. Harrison was instrumental in cosigning Mark bringing me in, because I'd done a few workouts with him in the summer when I was at Providence, and he knew I could help his game. So I was working with him on different stuff every day, and I could see Rick Carlisle looking at me a little funny. Rick was our head coach, and I *love* Rick, but it's hilarious that of all the head coaches of all the teams in the league that I could've coached under, Rick Carlisle gotta be the most *no-nonsense* coach imaginable. So Rick is watching me training Harrison, his star player, and let's just say my methods are . . . *unorthodox*.

Like, I don't know what you're picturing in your head when you're thinking about a ball handling coach. It's not like we're playing *NBA 2K*. We're not in the gym and I'm teaching you how to do *moves*. "Yo, take two dribbles to the right, then press L2 and circle, dog."

Nah. That's not what a good *handle* is, in real life. You can't plan on doing certain moves on a basketball court. Everything has to happen organically. So that's how I train you—totally off the cuff.

I mean, I could teach anybody how to dribble. I could teach a dolphin. I could teach anybody how to do "The Shammgod" in three minutes while I'm eating an egg and cheese bagel. It's nothing. But true *handle* is not about moves. It's about imagination. It's about creativity. It's about divine inspiration. So my goal when I'm training you is to *free you*. I'm going to make you so comfortable in uncomfortable situations that you don't even have to think out there, even when they're pressing you. Even when they're double-teaming you. Even when you got problems at home. Even when your people are asking you for $10,000 and you got problems with your baby mother and the coach don't like you. You're not thinking about any of that. You're not even thinking about the ball being in your hands. You're just *floating*. You're completely free. But how do we get you there? How do we get you levitating?

First, you gotta fall on your ass. Coach Shamm gotta break you down.

Mannnn, listen. I'm not coaching from the sidelines with binoculars. I'm out there on the floor *killing* these dudes. I got the NFL lineman tackling dummy strapped to my hands, and I'm *beating* on these NBA dudes while they try to get into the lane. I'm barking at them like Harlem killers used to bark at me, telling them they're gonna be in the G-League next spring. I'm hip-checking them like Gary Payton used to hip-check me. We're *battling*.

If we're training, I'm not teaching you moves, 99.9 percent of the time. I'm getting you so confident with that leather in your hands that you never even think about losing it, even when the lights are bright and you got the TNT cameras on you. You can't even entertain the idea of failure. All you're thinking about is where your body is going next, and in a split second you're already gone. It's automatic. It's *easy*, because you're just playing random NBA niggas. You're not in the gym with Shamm, getting the living hell beat out of you.

Now it's a piece of cake. Now it's a *relief* to be playing in an NBA game with the Gatorade breaks and the $30 million subs giving you a rest. With me, we not sitting down till we two *puddles*, kid.

Now we're getting better, see? But the thing is, you can't really get better without bumping your head first. And one random night, we were playing on the road somewhere, and Harrison bumped his head.

He got stripped while he was doing a move he normally wouldn't do, and Coach Carlisle was on my *ass* after the game.

"Do not be teaching him that stuff! This is not street basketball! This is the NBA!"

I'm sitting there just taking it, thinking: *Man, I didn't even teach him that move. He just pulled it out of the bag on his own.*

I went back to the hotel that night wondering how long I was going to be there. But I knew I just had to be patient. If I was Rick, I would've said the same thing. So me and Harrison kept on working, and a few weeks later, we played Charlotte, and he was absolutely going *off*. He was putting the ball behind his back, throwing it between his legs, doing step-back threes, just destroying the Hornets. And after the game, I see Rick in the locker room, and he's just shaking his head and laughing, like, "Okay. I see what's going on. Okay. I get it now."

Me and Rick's journey together is a beautiful thing. When I got to Dallas, he literally didn't know who the hell I was, or why I was there. Maybe a year into me being on his staff, he came up to me in the hallway one day, and he's almost *pointing* at me and smiling, like he's meeting a celebrity for the first time or something.

He goes, "Man, I didn't know who you *were*."

I said, "What do you mean, Coach?"

"I mean, I knew you played in the NBA, and I knew the way the players talked about you. But I didn't know the backstory. Then I watched this thing on YouTube about you last night."

I was cracking up.

I said, "Yeah, I get that a lot. The other night, my thirteen-year-old son found some old clips of me from March Madness and he was like: 'Man, dad. You were like . . . *Really good*.'"

Rick thought that was the funniest thing in the world.

He was like, "You're a *legend*. But I had no idea, because you don't act like that around here. Why didn't you say something?"

I said, "Man, I'm the same as everybody else. Two years ago, I was cleaning up towels. I'm just happy to be here teaching."

"You know what's so crazy about you? I've been in this league a long time, and I've never seen anything like it."

"What's that?"

"All the *agents* like you. The agents don't like anybody."

That was the beginning of another beautiful friendship. Me and Rick, we're the Odd Couple. But that's my boy. To this day, every time I run into him, he calls me "Legend."

We were building something special at the time, even if we weren't doing much winning. We were building a "We" culture.

We were setting the stage for greatness, you feel me? And then we got a blessing. In 2018, we drafted a generational talent out of Slovenia named Luka Dončić. As soon as I saw this dude come over as a nineteen-year-old, I knew I was looking at somebody who could be one of the greatest NBA players of all time. He was raw, but he loved the game of basketball, and everything you told him, he was just a sponge. When you get a player like that in your building, your only job is to not screw them up.

The truth is, NBA players are who they are. That's the biggest misconception from people who don't really know ball. It ain't rocket science, when it comes to player development. By the time these kids are coming to you in the NBA at nineteen years old, they've already played their ten thousand hours of basketball. If it's a veteran coming over, and they're twenty-six, they're pretty much set in stone. Your job as a coach is simply to make them a little bit better, and not a little bit worse. Technically, you're not going to make a night-and-day difference. But mentally? You can do a *lot*. That can be the difference between a playoff team and a champion. You have to let these guys unlock the greatness within themselves. But for that to happen, you need a real, authentic, honest culture, and that's what we were building in Dallas.

For my first five seasons as a coach, it was the *beautiful struggle*. We missed the playoffs three years in a row, and then Dirk retired. We rebuilt with a young squad, but then Covid hit, and the world turned upside down for a minute, and we got bounced in the first round by the Clippers two years in a row. Who's the Greek homie with the big boulder? Sisyphus? That's what we were doing. Pushing it up the hill. Falling back down. Pushing it back up. The process was the *point*. We were building something. Then in the summer of 2021, God put another NBA legend in my life. (I'm really getting greedy now, I know.) Rick Carlisle resigned, and the Mavs hired Jason Kidd, one of the greatest point guards of all time, as our new head coach. To be honest with you, I didn't know what that meant for me. A lot of coaches come in with their own staff, and they clean house. I could have easily been typing up the first resume I ever had to make in my life, but God had other plans. J-Kidd saw what I was trying to do right away, and he empowered me to be even more of a voice in the room. Even *more* of a truth-telling motherfucker.

We made it to the Western Conference Finals in 2022, when nobody believed in us. That's when Luka became *Luka*. Everybody in the world saw what we saw the first time he walked into our gym. We had an absolute *dog* in Jalen Brunson at the point. Just the ultimate competitor, who brought it every single night. On paper we didn't look like a contender. But we had such a tight culture, and we made it further than anybody expected. Unfortunately, we ran into Golden State in the Western Conference Finals, and they had the experience of a champion. Peak Steph? Peak Klay? Peak Iggy and Draymond? They beat us in five, and it was a learning experience for us. The next season, we lost Brunson in free agency, and we had some tough injuries, and we missed the playoffs. Sisyphus, son. The boulder rolled back down the hill.

But we made a move that season that brought another ONE OF ONE into my life. We didn't just trade for any point guard. We traded for the man with the most natural handle in NBA *history*, in my humble opinion. Kyrie Irving. The purest dribbler I've ever seen. And now I was blessed to go to work with him every day. But it goes a lot deeper than that, like everything in my story. The craziest part about Ky is that his father Drederick grew up in the Bronx. He was ten years older than me, and everybody knew Drederick in the hood, because he could really ball. Well, guess who grew up in the same housing project building as Drederick? *Tiny Archibald*, my PE teacher, the man who introduced me to dribbling, and one of the greatest to ever play point guard in the NBA.

Don't let anybody ever tell you that New York City ain't the birthplace of the Point God. It's in the tap water.

At the time Ky came to us, it felt like the whole world was using him as a scapegoat. Not just for his stance on the Covid vaccine stuff, but for a lot of things. In our league, it's always a soap opera. The media builds you up and then they tear you down—just so they can build you back up again as a redemption story. That's the game. After we got Ky, it took us a minute to click. We went 9–18 the rest of that season, and the talking heads were *roasting* us. Not just Ky but Luka and J-Kidd and our whole front office. We had our fifteen minutes of shame. We were the momentary villains. When the spotlight is on you like that, it can divide a locker room.

I remember J-Kidd let me give a speech to the team near the end of that season, and I just tried to draw on everything I ever learned in my life—about me, Mase, Cam, my mother, Harlem, failure, everything. I said, "Y'all need to give each other some *grace.* I know you sit there and look at the man across from you and think that he don't go through *nothing.* Like he got it all. Like he don't have any problems. Every motherfucker in this room got problems. You think Luka don't have stress? A kid who comes over here at nineteen, who has to be the face of a whole *country?* You think Ky don't have any stress? A guy who is just trying to play ball, who got the media painting a picture of him that's the opposite of who he really is? Come on, man. This is a fucking *we* thing. We all got problems. We have to be in this together, otherwise what's the point?"

As I started speaking up more, people took notice, and I got a promotion that I didn't even know existed. Mark named me an assistant coach as head of player culture. It was the first position of its kind in the NBA. And it was perfect, because I always felt like my real job, way more than just teaching guys how to dribble, was teaching them to see the big picture. In basketball, the picture is always super small. It's in size 8 print in a box score, you feel me? You shot 20 percent from three. You had 4 turnovers. Some random dude on the internet made a joke about you with a picture of SpongeBob or whatever. Who cares? That's kiddie shit. That's small. That's infinitesimal in the grand scheme of life. But try telling that to a twenty-three-year-old kid who gets all his self-worth from what they sayin' on a *telephone.*

I've been shot at in *real life.* I've been broke in *real life.* I've been sleeping on the streets in *real life.* It ain't theoretical for me and real dudes like me. So I feel like when I speak to these guys, my words actually resonate. I tell my guys all the time, until they're sick of hearing me: it's never as good as you think, and it's never as bad as you think. The worst day of your life? Yo, in ten years, that can be the day that made you who you are now.

Why did I make it out the hood? Because of the worst day of my life, when I was grabbing kitchen knives to protect my mother and sleeping on a bench in an alleyway.

Why did I make it to the NBA? Because everybody I knew was either getting killed or getting locked up.

Why did I become an overseas legend? Because I got cut from the NBA after twenty games, and I had no other choice but to get money by any means necessary to keep my son in diapers.

Why did I become an NBA coach? Because I was picking up towels off the floor of a locker room at thirty-four years old.

Your worst day can be your first day. The start of a new chapter. The beginning of your revenge tour, you feel me?

I remember sitting with Ky before that next 2023–24 season, and I knew he felt like the whole world was beating up on him.

But I told him the truth, because what else am I gonna do?

I said, "Man, you can't be misunderstood if you're not trying to let people understand you."

I don't know if that's any kind of deep insight, but I really felt like it resonated with him.

I said, "Don't worry. Once we finish this season, everybody is going to spin the block. They're all going to come back like they always loved you."

Ky is one of those people that I feel like I've met already in another lifetime. When we play one-on-one or we're just sitting around the gym, 98 percent of what we talk about has nothing to do with basketball. We talk about gratitude and gratefulness. How many superstars you know talk about gratitude? How many millionaires you know talk about gratefulness? Ky is built different. I think that's why he's so polarizing to fans. He's a curious, intelligent man who just so happens to be naturally blessed with a basketball in his hands. Some people hate that. Do you ever notice how kids *love* Ky? What does that tell you?

Watching him play basketball is like watching a true artist paint a painting. Forget *dribbling* for a second. Don't watch his hands. It's all an illusion. It's the negative space. Watch Ky's feet and his body control movement and his angles to the basket. That's the paint. It's what he does after the dribble that makes him an artist. He taps so deep inside himself that he has no fear of failure, and he's able to improvise the impossible. He's flowing. He's water.

What does a great novelist tell you about a book?

"The story has a life of its own."

What does a great jazz artist tell you about music?

"I go where the muse takes me."

It's the same with a transcendent dribbler. When nothing is planned, everything is possible. You free your mind, and you let the muse lead the way.

After you do something impossible on the court, the media is going to ask you, "How did you do that?"

And you're going to tell the truth.

"I don't know."

That's an artist. That's Kyrie Irving.

By the middle of that season, I knew we had something good going on. I knew because the guys were comfortable enough to give *me* a ton of shit too. It was a truth-telling culture all around. See, these NBA buffets hit different. I was so used to eating the college cafeteria buffets. But now I'm in Mark Cuban's world, and in Mark Cuban's world we got a whole *squad* of private chefs cooking up the steaming salmon and the organic broccoli and the little mini wagyu burgers straight from Japan and those crispy little fingerling potatoes and shit. You know what I'm talking about? Those little potatoes where the outside is super crispy and the inside is fluffy and perfect? We're a long way from the Providence Dining Hall tater tots. So I'm not gonna lie, I was getting *hefty*, man.

And of course, your truth-telling never extends to your own number on that scale, right? So in my mind, I'm lying to myself. I'm looking in the mirror like: I'm getting diesel, man. This *all muscle*. I'm looking like 50 Cent. *Get Rich or Die Tryin'* 50. Where my durag?

I was playing myself.

Then I showed up to shootaround one day, and I took my shirt off, and Marquise Morris and Ky were just shaking their heads.

Ky said, "Oh, you're getting comfortable. You're getting *too comfortable*, Shamm."

I said, "Huh? What you mean?"

Marquise said, "Man, you're getting *soft*. You pushing three hundred pounds?"

I said, "Huhhhh? Come on, son. That's crazy. I'm two thirty!"

I got on the scale when I got back to the hotel and I was 275. I'm shifting the scale around on the floor, like, *Nah, something's wrong with the calibration.*

Nope. I was 275. It was January 1, 2024.

I went back the next day and I told Ky and Marquise, "Alright. You right. You right. But I'm gonna drop fifty pounds by the end of March."

They were cracking up. They said, "You not gonna drop fifty pounds. That's impossible. I seen you at dinner, Shamm."

I said, "Okay, Imma drop seventy."

"Whatever, man. Come on."

"Watch me."

"Okay."

"Funny, right? We'll see what's funny. And I ain't need no Ozempic. This is gonna be all natural."

"Seventy?"

"Seventy."

Mannnnnn. These boys didn't know *who I am*. You never play around with me when I say I'm gonna do something. Just like when I was fourteen years old and I wanted to make McDonald's All-American, I *snapped*.

Play my damn music, man!

(2Pac's "Hit 'Em Up" plays while I'm eating carrots with no ranch dressing.)

Dog, I snapped. I'd wake up at five o'clock in the morning and speed-walk on the treadmill for two hours so I could be showered and ready for meetings at eight. Then I'd work the guys out like normal for two hours, go to the cafeteria and eat like a thimble full of tuna and a leaf of arugula, do all my meetings and prep, then it would be 4 p.m. I'd be looking at that cookie and brownie station and gripping the wood on the desk with my fucking veins popping out, but I never caved. I'd do my hot yoga before the games, then after the games I'd be on the treadmill again for another two hours.

After a month, I'm walking into the team meetings and Ky and Marquise are looking at each other *buggin'*.

"Yo, Shamm. You serious about this?"

"Watch me."

After two months, I'm walking into the team meetings, and *everybody* is buggin'.

"Yo, Shamm. You skinny as *hell*. You down like thirty pounds."

"Forty-four."

By March 31, the guys put me on the scale in the weight room, and everybody was going crazy, like I just won the dunk competition or something.

The scale read 204. I lost 71 pounds in three months.

Marquise was like, "Man, how is that even possible?"

I said, "Let me ask you a question. How does a kid who doesn't even know how to dribble a basketball at twelve years old become a McDonald's All-American five years later?"

"I dunno. How?"

"Discipline. Match mine and we gonna do great things."

The whole rest of that season, and all through the playoffs, we were on one of those magical runs, like the one we went on at Providence in '97. We beat my old friend Ty Lue and the Clippers in Round 1. And then in Round 2, we were heavy underdogs to the Thunder, but Luka took over the series and we advanced to the Western Conference Finals against the Timberwolves.

I'll never forget, right before Game 1, Anthony Edwards told the media, "I got Kyrie." I guess he was trying to make a statement or give his team some juice or something. But it gave *us* juice instead. I remember standing around the locker room watching the clip and everybody was just looking at one another like: "Huh?"

We knew what Ky was about to do.

He went out in Game 1 and put everybody on roller skates. He dropped 13 points in the first *quarter*. I'd never seen him so aggressive. He reminded the world exactly who he is, and we took Game 1.

Then in Game 2, it was Luka's turn. Now, what you have to understand is, me and Luka had been working on something for *six years*. For some reason, he could never do a right step-back. I was on his ass for six whole years about it. This man's game has it all, but it was almost like an inside joke: "Luka can't do a right step-back." We worked on it and worked on it, and he could do it in practice all the time, but he'd never pull it out in a game.

So flash forward to the end of Game 2, with control of the series on the line, and Minnesota is up two with twelve seconds left in the game. Luka gets the ball at the top of the key. And yo— just like with me in March Madness '97 when I pulled out the Shammgod, what happens? They switch the big man onto him. Rudy Gobert hops up on him. Defensive Player of the Year.

Ten-million-foot wingspan. But what's every big fella's weakness? The feet. You gotta cross him up and get him off balance. And what does Luka do? It's just like we practiced ten thousand times in the gym, when nobody was watching. He fakes right and goes left. But when Rudy tries to catch up with him, he goes between his legs and *back* to his right again. Then Rudy tries to catch up again, and this is the key moment that you're not going to appreciate unless you really understand basketball, or you watch a super-slow-motion replay: Luka takes *one* dribble like he's going to the basket. That's what causes Rudy's knees to buckle. That's what buys Luka the half second of space to get the shot off. That's pure imagination. That's an artist in full flow.

Luka hops behind the arc for the step-back three.

Ball is in the air.

Twenty thousand people holding their breath.

The feeling we live for.

The freeze frame.

Popcorn flying in the air.

Mouths hanging open.

Splash.

Money.

Game.

Crowd goes bananas.

The first thing Luka said to me when we got to the locker room was "Man, we worked on that, Shamm! We worked on that!"

I said, "Yeah, but that's the first time I ever seen you actually *do it*. You were saving it, huh?"

In the biggest moment on the biggest stage in basketball, something that I taught somebody made that tiny little .005 percent difference. To me, that feeling was more fulfilling than anything I ever did on a court with the ball in my own hands. Basketball gave me everything good in my life. When I was back to sleeping in my car and picking up dirty towels, I made a promise to myself that if I ever got a chance to be a coach, my only mission was to leave the game a little bit better than I found it.

That season, with Ky and Luka and our run to the NBA Finals, I finally felt like I had accomplished that goal. Winning wasn't the whole point. Of course, we wanted to beat the Boston Celtics and raise the trophy with the confetti and the tears and the champagne showers. Ever since you're a little kid, or in my case, a teenager, that's exactly what you dream of. We got real close, and we didn't quite get it done. But there's dreams and then there's real life. And real life unfolds how it's supposed to unfold. Boston won the series in five, because they honestly deserved it a little bit more than we did. We had the heart of a champion. They had the experience of one.

Sometimes you just have to sit in that pain and let it fuel you.

As I've gotten older, I've learned to not shy away from any emotion of life. When I was young, I was just numb to everything. That was my defense mechanism. But life is about growing and evolving, and even a real nigga like me can talk to a therapist.

Now, I don't try to mask the pain *or* the joy. Whatever God wants for me, that's what it's going to be that day. I wanted to win that title as bad as anybody, but sometimes you have to zoom out.

You gotta take the God's-eye view. I think about that night when the security guard found me sleeping in my car. I remember I was reclined way back, listening to the radio and looking at the stars through the sunroof. In New York City, you can never really see the stars. They're hidden most nights, if you even remember to look up. But in Providence, you see the heavens for real. So I looked up, trying to get myself to nod off to sleep in the cold, and I thought: *Dang, these are the same stars I was looking at when I was nine years old on the bench in the alleyway. Think of everything you've won and lost since then, Shamm. Think of all the joy and the pain, man. These stars have been up there, unchanged, looking down on Harlem, looking down on China, looking down on you. Did you do good? Did you hold up your end of the bargain? Is this really the end of your story?*

I looked at the millions of stars frozen up there in the sky, and I talked to God again.

Just show me the way.

Just give me a chance.

When God talks to you, it's not words. It's a sensation.

And that sensation told me: *Just keep going.*

Twelve years after I was sleeping in my car and cleaning up towels, I made it to the NBA Finals. If I knew then what my life would be like now, I'd have thought it was a fairy tale. God blessed me with two more sons, Easton and Justice, when I came to Dallas. I got a whole starting five of Shammgods *and* a sixth man. I got an amazing wife, Crystal, and we live in a big house with grass as far as the eye can see, like we on *Green Acres*, son. My fourteen-year-old goes to a school where he leaves his iPad sitting out on the bleachers when he goes to the bathroom. I'm looking at him like: Yo, do you even know how I grew up? You just left $1,200 sitting out unattended. If I wasn't your father, I'd be about to *rob* your ass, dummy.

He's *soft*. All my sons are soft. And ain't that a beautiful thing? How can I not be grateful?

My youngest son, Justice, he wakes up in the morning and the first thing he says to me with his bed head and his big smile is, "Hey, I love you dad! I got the best dad in the woooorrrrlllllddd!!!"

I get nervous sending this little dude to kindergarten because he's got such a pure soul. I don't want anybody corrupting him.

I wake up every single day, and I just thank God.

I may not be an NBA champion. Yet. But I won *life*. I am at peace.

And you don't think it's all connected? Have you not been paying attention to this story?

After Game 5 of the 2023 finals, guess who was the *first person* the head coach of the Boston Celtics came over to hug when the confetti was coming down, and they were NBA champions? Jason Tatum? Jaylen Brown? Ky? Luka? Nah.

The coach of the Boston Celtics went to hug the player development coach for the Dallas Mavericks.

Why in the world was Joe Mazzulla hugging God Shammgod?

You already know, man. I'm the black Forrest Gump. Me and Joe, our relationship goes deep. I was actually the first person Joe texted when the Celtics wanted to hire him. He coached college ball at Fairmont State, and guess who played for Fairmont State?

The kid who was raised in a basketball gym. The kid who was at every one of my games since he was two weeks old. The kid who saved my life. My son, God Shammgod Jr.

Joe texted me some questions about the NBA and then he asked me point-blank, "How should I handle this?"

I told him, "Take the job."

All of this, it was all written. Both of our paths were leading us to that moment.

Joe called me up one day out of the blue a few weeks after the finals.

He said, "I always loved your son as a player, so I wanted you to be the first one to know. I'm gonna hire him to be a part of our staff in Boston."

I said, "Really?"

He said, "Really."

Forget being a street legend. Forget doing "The Shammgod." Forget getting drafted. Forget my comeback story. Forget it all, man.

That right there was the single proudest moment of my life.

I had fulfilled my promise to God.

I held up my end of the bargain.

I had raised a good man.

What is the meaning of life?

Do you ever ask yourself that question? I'm not being funny. What are we all doing here? Sit with that question for a minute and really answer me.

Is the point to make money? I had money. I lost money. I have money again. It's cool. It ain't the meaning. Is the point to be famous? I've been famous in the hood and in America and all the way over in China. It's cool. It ain't the meaning. Is the point to live out your wildest dreams? I've lived mine, for real. I've played in Madison Square Garden. I've coached in the NBA Finals. I've become friends with every NBA legend and celebrity you can think of. Puma gave me my own signature shoe at *forty-five years old*. Who gets their own sneaker at forty-five? *Me*, who else? But all that pride, all that ego stuff . . . It's cool. But it still ain't the point. It's definitely not the meaning of life.

The meaning of life . . .

I think it's closer to what happened when I got a phone call a few years back, just out of the blue.

Kobe called me. I hadn't talked to him in a minute. In life, you lose track of people a little bit. That's just human nature. It's not that you grow apart. It's more like your lives run in parallel, you feel me? It's the same with me and Mase, Cam, Steph, Kevin Jackson, everybody. Life has a way of bringing you back together again when the time is right, and it's like a day hasn't gone by. You pick up right where you left off. When I see Mase now, it's the same Mase I knew when we were kids. It doesn't matter that he's a pastor now. For me, he's the kid from PS92, and he always will be. When I see Cam, he's still the same hilarious Cam from the Delanor Projects wearing the pink bucket hat and the fur coat to the party. But sometimes, years go by without you connecting in real life, because that's just how it goes. You shoot a text: *You good?* And that's the extent of it.

With me and Kobe, it was the same thing. I was following what he was doing as a father, coaching his girls, and I was just so happy for him. But I was always on the road with the Mavs, and we hadn't caught up in years.

Then in 2019, somebody told me that Kobe was looking for my new number. I gave it to them to pass on to him, and the next day, I got this call from a California area code.

I thought it was probably Kobe, but when I answered, the dude was talking just like *Jordan*.

I'm not even being funny. Me and MJ are cool, so I thought it was MJ for a second.

He's like, "How you doing, Shamm? Everything good?"

I said, "Kobe?"

THE WORD OF GOD

He said, "Yeah, it's *Kob*."

I said, "Man, after all these years, you still trying to be MJ! I literally thought I was talking to Mike!"

He was cracking up. He asked me if I had any free time in the off-season to train out in California. I thought he was talking about training *him* for a second. But then he said, "I got about six or seven girls out here from my daughter's team, and I want you to work them out. But I mean *really* work them out. Do you think you got the time?"

I said, "Man, I always got time for you."

So the first week of the offseason, Kobe flew me out to LA. And of course, everything was done in true Kobe fashion. The driver picked me up at the airport, and as soon as I got to my hotel, Kobe was waiting for me in the lobby with this full itinerary. Like, he's got this shit printed out in a spiral binder and everything. He gives me a hug, and then he immediately switches right into dad mode. He's like, "Alright, so I got everything listed here. Every session. Plus lunch breaks. Recovery. Now listen, don't take it easy on these girls, alright?"

I said, "*Aight*, Kob. I hear you."

"They're here to work."

"*Aight*, Kob. I got you."

"We start early. Six a.m."

Now I'm getting *flashbacks*, man. I'm having PTSD from ABCD. I'm remembering being at camp with this dude, and I'm thinking: *Yo, this is about to be* hilarious. *I can't wait to see this man as a Basketball Dad. He's gonna be* buggin'.

He's tapping the paper, like, "First session is six to eight. Then we break for lunch. You can nap or whatever. Then the second session is twelve to two."

"*Aight*, Kob. We good! No stress! See you at six."

But yo—I had *seen* this movie before. I know if I show up to that gym at 5:59 a.m., Kobe and all these girls are gonna be in there already in a full sweat, lined up in the North Korean military roll-call line, laughing at me in front of all these girls, like, "Well, well, well. Look who rolled out of bed and decided to join us."

So I set my alarm for 5:20.

(I don't got the Casio clock anymore. It's that soothing iPhone alarm.)

So the soothing iPhone alarm is going off the next morning, and I get dressed and head over to the gym.

I'm having déjà vu now. I'm walking over to the gym with my book bag, and just like twenty-five years ago, the sun is still not up yet, and I'm just grumbling to myself like, "Yo, we talking about middle school girls, man. They wanna sleep in. They're not *about this life* yet, man. They're no way they gonna be in this—"

Oh hell naw.

I heard 'em before I seen 'em.

Doot-doot-doot-doot-doot.

Doot-doot-doot-doot-doot. Doot-doot-doot-doot-doot.

Doot-doot-doot-doot-doot.

Everybody knows that echo.

I open the double doors, and I got seven chipper girls already doing stretches and jumping jacks and shit. I got Kobe already in a full sweat, with the whistle around his neck, smiling at me from ear to ear. I got all these girls' *parents* already in the gym, sitting in the bleachers with the picnic basket, waving at me and shit, like, "Mornin', Coach!"

I felt like I was hallucinating. Yo, it's 5:45 in the morning. Who loves basketball this much? Where's the hidden cameras? They're playing with me.

Kobe's daughter Gigi literally *sprints* up to me, with this huge smile on her face, like, "Hi, Coach Shamm! Me and my dad watch all your stuff on YouTube! Are you gonna show us how to—"

I'm still trying to wipe the crust out of my eyes, son.

I'm like, "Yo, just give me one second, Gigi. I gotta lace up my shoes."

Kobe is pointing at me in front of all the parents, and he's like, "See, you know I love this guy, because I let him in here with Pumas on."

Everybody's laughing. Dude is doing stand-up comedy at five thirty in the morning.

He's in full basketball-dad mode with the parents. He gets the girls sitting in that tight cross-legged circle around him, and he's telling the parents, "This is the guy who taught me how to dribble. We're so lucky to have him here, so let's have a good day today. *Work* on three."

"One, two, three . . . *work*."

I'm just looking at him and shaking my head. It was a beautiful thing to see, man. He was loving life. He got his second act.

Even the way the morning sunlight was coming in the windows of the gym that day and hitting the hardwood, it felt unreal.

When I say that basketball is a sanctuary, I think of that day. That gym was full of love. Pure love. For two hours, all we did was dribble. We didn't put up a single shot. And every single one of those girls *loved* it. When we took a break for lunch, Gigi didn't want to go eat. She wanted to stay in the gym and ask me questions about all these different moves she saw me do on YouTube.

I remember all the girls were sitting on the bleachers getting water and changing their shoes, and they were telling me how they were all gonna go to the same college together. It was exactly like me and Mase sitting on the fence at Rucker Park, dreaming. It was exactly like me and Steph sitting on the pavement in Coney Island, dreaming.

"We're gonna be at Georgia Tech together, man."

"Who gets to wear Kenny Anderson's number twelve?"

Only it was . . .

"We're all gonna go play at UConn together."

"If Geno wants one of us, he's gonna have to take all of us."

"We're all gonna live in the same dorm."

"You gonna come see us play, Coach Shamm?"

All those girls wanted to do was talk basketball with me and ask me about Luka and Dirk and Kyrie and Ja and all these guys that I was blessed to come across in my life. On the surface, you might think we got nothing in common. I'm a forty-three-year-old man from Harlem. They're twelve-year-old girls from California. But it's like we were all friends in another lifetime. We shared a deep connection. A profound love for the game of basketball.

Kobe finally had to come over and tell them they had to go get lunch.

"Don't worry, Coach Shamm got another session for you at twelve. He'll be here when you get back."

I went to my hotel to take a power nap, and when I came back to the gym, I asked Kobe, "Alright, what do you want me to show them now?"

He said, "What are you talking about?"

I said, "We just dribbled for two hours. You want me to show them some passing drills?"

He said, "No. We're *dribbling*."

I'm looking at him like, "Bro, I train NBA guys that can only go forty-five minutes. They *grown men* with personal chefs. These girls are gonna dribble for *four hours*?"

And he's looking at me back like we're still seventeen years old, like, "Yeah, dog. These girls are gonna dribble for *four hours*. What's the problem?"

In the back of my head, I'm thinking, *This dude is still as crazy as ever, man. These girls are gonna come back all lackadaisical from the carbs. Ain't no sixth grader in the world who wanna dribble for four hours. We gonna be playing H-O-R-S-E by 12:45.*

Mannnnnn. These girls come back from lunch and they're *running* onto the court.

"What we doing now, Coach Shamm?!"

"We . . . we dribbling."

"Wooooohooooo!"

Oh my GOD. I'm racking my brain, like: *Yo, I don't know if I have enough* shit *to show these girls for another two hours.* I'm trying to think of new drills. Their energy is breaking my imagination. I'm telling them, "Alright, time-out. Coach Shamm needs to take a Gatorade break. Y'all *wild*. Luka can only do this for forty-five minutes before he wants to go check his Instagram. Y'all *crazy*."

Gigi would've stayed out there on that court all day. It was so funny, because she *walked* like Kobe. She *talked* like Kobe. She *chewed gum* like Kobe. She even had the tongue hanging out like Kobe when she shot her jumper. She was the Mini Mamba. I can close my eyes right now and see the look of pure joy on her face when she had a basketball in her hands. And I can see the way Kobe was looking at her, like he was so proud to be her father. That moment is eternal. It can never die.

And that is my answer to the question. The ultimate question. What is the meaning of life? What are we all doing here? What is our purpose?

It's love.

It's the feeling that we all shared in that gym.

That's the answer.

Love.

It's the feeling that I felt at PS92 in Harlem, when Mase showed me how to dribble a basketball for the first time.

It's the feeling that I felt at the Rucker, sitting up in that tree overlooking the court with my friends, having my mind blown for the first time by the Terminator and Pookie and Mike Boogie and all the streetball players.

It's the feeling that I had when I was all by myself, dribbling at 145th Street Park in the middle of the night, imagining that I was playing at Madison Square Garden, trying to shake my own shadow.

It's the feeling I had when I held my son in my arms after every high school game, or when my mother hugged me after the McDonald's Game and told me, "You're so amazing, what you do with that ball."

It's the feeling I had when I stood in the crowd and I watched Mase perform at the Apollo Theater.

It's the feeling I had every time I was in the gym at six o'clock in the morning with my guys at Providence, just sweating it out before practice, pushing them to live their dreams.

It's the feeling I have when I see any one of my six children laughing and feeling free, not having to worry about the things I had to worry about when I was a kid.

It's the feeling I have every time I feel the leather in my hands.

Love. I felt it that day with Kobe and Gigi and them girls as purely and as clearly as I've ever felt it. We weren't just in a gym. We were in heaven.

Eight months later, Kobe was gone. Gigi was gone. A lot of the girls in that gym were gone.

It was incomprehensible.

I remember I was in the locker room with the Mavs before practice on January 26, 2020, and everybody's phones started blowing up with rumors about Kobe and a helicopter crash. Nobody believed it. It had to be fake. Kobe could never die. He's just one of those people. He's invincible. People were showing me tweets and text messages, and I literally didn't believe it for a second.

But then I ran into Rick Carlisle in the hallway, and it looked like he'd seen a ghost. His voice was shaking. He said, "I just talked to somebody. And I think it's true."

I still didn't believe it. They got something wrong. They get things wrong all the time. It's all just a mistake, man. Somebody is playing a sick joke. Kobe ain't gone.

I said, "Man, slow down. Let me call his assistant. I'm gonna clear this up. This has gotten crazy."

So I called Kobe's assistant.

She actually picked up the phone, and for a split second, I thought: *See? This is crazy* . . .

Then she just started screaming. And that's when I knew.

She said, "He's gone. They're gone."

I collapsed on the floor and I just started crying. Rick was hugging me. I was rolling around in physical pain. It felt like the world was over. It didn't feel real to me for months. Years. It still doesn't feel real to me.

I have lived on this earth for almost fifty years now. I've been all over the world. I've lived four different lives. And I don't know too much for certain. All I know for sure is that death is not the end. I know that we will all meet again. I know it, because the moment that I met Kobe, I knew we had met already in another life. The moment I met Gigi and those girls, I knew that we were old friends.

If you don't believe me, that's fine. Maybe you haven't lived a real life yet. But when you've been around the block like I have, you see the pattern in things.

We will meet again, around the way.

Until then, I keep them alive in my soul. Not just Kobe and

Gigi and all those girls, but my mother, who passed on a few years ago. Everybody who left us too soon. Biggie and Chief and Black Widow and Big L and Hudie and Steph's father, and Ron Carlos, and so many other people whose names you don't even know. People who helped me get out of the hood and live my dreams.

I keep them alive by telling my story. Their story. *Our* story. The Harlem story. The basketball story. The story of our culture.

They live on in eternity, because we take them with us everywhere we go, as long as we still got those vivid memories. Any time I'm feeling down, like I don't want to answer that 6 a.m. alarm when we're on a long road trip, like I'm tired of the business of basketball, like I just want to relax and hit the snooze button, like I want to get too comfortable, like I want to take this life for granted . . . man, I just think of Gigi Bryant ready and waiting in that gym at 5:45 with a big smile on her face.

Just radiating joy and positivity and the love of the game.

What did I tell you? The earth spins twice. Do you believe me now?

To her father, when he was young, I was: "Shammgod, Shammgod, Shammgod. This is what Shammgod can do."

To her, twenty-five years later, I was: "Coach Shamm, Coach Shamm, Coach Shamm! Is this a little better? How do my feet look? How 'bout this? Is this better? Is this better?"

I think about that memory now, and it makes me cry.

But it's not tears of sadness. Nah, not at all. It's tears of pure joy. Because I got to fulfill my ultimate destiny: I got to leave the game a little better than I found it. I got to give back. I got to be a *teacher*.

It's an unlikely story, I know.

I came into this cold world as a young kid in Harlem, growing up around the projects during the crack era, thrown to the wolves. Getting my burgers snatched, getting jumped over three bucks, running from gunshots, just trying to stay alive. Not even safe in my own home. Clutching a knife under my pillow some nights, just trying to protect my mother. Staring up at the stars in the alley, just asking God for a way out.

Nobody would've bet on me. But basketball saved my life.

And I know that when my body leaves this world one day, my spirit will still live on through the game.

My name will still ring out. Shammgod will still be around, whenever you hear that booming echo on the pavement. In the rain, in the cold, in the snow, in the middle of the night, in every park, in every hood . . .

Doot-doot-doot-doot.

Doot-doot-doot-doot.

Doot-doot-doot-doot.

Whenever you see a kid at the park all alone, standing under a lone streetlight—the last *good* streetlight that's still flickering—whenever you see that lonely kid just trying over and over and over again to shake their shadow, I hope that you'll think of a young broke kid from Harlem.

Forty years ago, I lay on a bench in an alleyway in Harlem, looked up at the stars, and asked for God to give me a chance.

The gift that he gave me was not money. It was not fame.

It was not even basketball.

It was love.

I look back on this impossible journey, and all I can do is thank the people God put in my life who looked out for a young broke kid in a cold world.

Some of them were street legends. Some of them were NBA legends. Some of them were gangsters and preachers and teachers. But most of them were just regular people with love in their hearts.

When you are given a gift, it's your duty to pay it back to the universe.

Now I am the teacher.

Forty years ago, God spoke to me, clear as day.

But you can't reply to God in words. It would never do it justice, right?

So my reply is an echo. It's the echo of the streets, son. The eternal echo. Leather on concrete.

Doot-doot-doot-doot.

Doot-doot-doot-doot.

Doot-doot-doot-doot.

"Is that better, Shamm?"

Doot-doot-doot-doot.

Doot-doot-doot-doot.

Doot-doot-doot-doot.

ACKNOWLEDGMENTS

Adrienne Wells

God Shammgod Sr.

Prince

Shammquanna

Tanaya

Elisha

Angel

Shamel

All my coaches

Harlem, New York City, for making me who I am

My wife and kids

La Salle Academy

Providence College

Washington Wizards

Dallas Mavericks

Mark Cuban

142nd Street

145th Street Park

Rucker Park

Kevin Jackson

Ron Carlos

Zig, Woods, Mase, Cam'ron, Howie

The Arnold family

Future

Kenny Anderson

OG Juan, Mousey, Norman, Jay

Minisink

Will and Ava Fullenweider

Early Kenneth McCray

Mike Bruno, BBO

Crystal Shammgod

Prince Shammgod

Justice Shammgod

Easton Shammgod

God Shammgod Jr.

Eryk Shammgod

Amir Shammgod

God Shammgod

ABOUT THE AUTHOR

God Shammgod is a former professional NBA player and basketball coach currently working with the Dallas Mavericks. He played with the Washington Wizards during the 1997–98 season after being drafted by them in the second round of the 1997 NBA draft. Despite a brief NBA career, he is well-known as the progenitor and namesake of a widely used crossover dribble, "The Shammgod."